When America Liked Ike

When America Liked Ike

How Moderates Won the 1952 Presidential Election and Reshaped American Politics

Gary A. Donaldson

ROWMAN & LITTLEFIELD
Lanham • Boulder • New York • London

Published by Rowman & Littlefield
A wholly owned subsidiary of The Rowman & Littlefield Publishing Group, Inc.
4501 Forbes Boulevard, Suite 200, Lanham, Maryland 20706
www.rowman.com

Unit A, Whitacre Mews, 26-34 Stannary Street, London SE11 4AB

British Library Cataloguing in Publication Information Available

Library of Congress Cataloging-in-Publication Data
ISBN 978-1-4422-1175-9 (cloth : alk. paper)
ISBN 978-1-4422-1177-3 (electronic)

♾™ The paper used in this publication meets the minimum requirements of American
National Standard for Information Sciences—Permanence of Paper for Printed Library
Materials, ANSI/NISO Z39.48-1992.

Printed in the United States of America

Contents

Abbreviations

ACLU	American Civil Liberties Union
ADA	Americans for Democratic Action
AES	Adlai E. Stevenson
AESP	Adlai E. Stevenson Papers, Princeton University
COHC	Columbia [University] Oral History Collection
DDE	Dwight David Eisenhower
DNC	Democratic National Committee/Convention
ELOHC	Eisenhower Library Oral History Collection
EP	Eisenhower Papers, Eisenhower Library, Abilene, Kansas
FDR	Franklin Delano Roosevelt
HST	Harry S. Truman
HSTL	Harry S. Truman Library, Independence, Missouri
HSTLOHC	Harry S. Truman Library Oral History Collection
HSTP	Harry S. Truman Papers
LBJ	Lyndon Baines Johnson
LBJA	Lyndon Baines Johnson Archives
LBJL	Lyndon Baines Johnson Library, Austin, Texas
LBJLOHC	Lyndon Baines Johnson Library Oral History Collection
LBJOC	Lyndon Baines Johnson Oral History Collection
MHS	Massachusetts Historical Society, Boston
NYT	*The New York Times*
PPP	Public Papers of the Presidents
RMNL	Richard M. Nixon Library, Loma Linda, California
RMNP	Richard M. Nixon Papers
RNC	Republican National Committee/Convention
U.N.	United Nations
WSHS	Wisconsin State Historical Society, Madison, Wisconsin

Introduction

What makes the 1952 campaign so important? Why write a book about it? Celebrated journalist Jon Meacham, in 2015, wrote a book about the administration of President George H. W. Bush, where he concludes that the current conflicts between the Democrats and the Republicans in Washington had their beginnings in 1989. That year, Newt Gingrich, the newly elected minority whip, represented the Republican Right. He confronted Bush—the then newly elected president of the United States and leader of the Republican moderates—sometimes called the "Establishment Republicans." The two, Meacham insists, clashed over policy. To Meacham, that was the origins of the current conflicts between the Republican Right and their moderate brethren.

In this book, I will argue that that conflict had its origins much earlier, at least as far back as the 1952 presidential election. That year, Eisenhower, a moderate among moderates, ran as a Republican. Running against him for the Republican nomination was Robert A. Taft, the son of a president and an ardent conservative. The Taft wing of the party clashed head on (and even dramatically) against the Eisenhower moderates. Taft died soon after the election, but the Taft wing of the party lived on for decades, followed in the Senate by Barry Goldwater in the mid-1960s, and then by Ronald Reagan through the 1980s. That wing of the Republican Party (the right wing, the Old Guard, and the Tea Party) has been around for decades, always pushing against the Republican moderates, always fighting what they called the "me-tooism" of the Eisenhower-Dewey-Rockefeller wing of the party.

The 1952 campaign was not, as some have argued, a party realignment, but it was a sharp political diversion, even a departure from the nature of American politics. The 1952 presidential campaign was the first election following the New Deal-Fair Deal era of American economic history. It was the

1

first election since 1928 in which an incumbent was not on the ticket. And it was the first election since 1932 in which Franklin Roosevelt (or his successor Harry Truman) did not run.

There was also a departure among the Democrats. Adlai Stevenson, the Democratic nominee, realized in 1952 that Truman, for several reasons, was not a popular figure, and that the wave of the future did not include the New Deal-Fair Deal philosophy of big government. Stevenson himself was not much of a Roosevelt New Dealer-type liberal. His response as the Democratic candidate in 1952 was to cut himself away from Truman, to get as far away from the Little Man from Missouri as possible. The Democratic Party then stopped being the party of the New Deal and the Fair Deal and started becoming something much more moderate, perhaps less liberal under Stevenson's moderation. Lyndon Johnson may have tried to bring back to the Democratic Party that old New Deal-Fair Deal purpose in the 1960s, but the time for that type of economic divergence had probably passed. If you are looking for a time when the New Deal-Fair Deal era came to an end, look no further than 1952; and if you are looking for a figure, a person, who was responsible for that end, look no further than Adlai Stevenson.

The 1952 campaign was also the first election since World War II (or at least the first election since the debacle of 1948).That means that the depression and the war, the two defining moments of the twentieth century, were both behind America. And Americans could look forward for the first time in decades, with a new outlook.

It was also the first campaign in which television played a part. Television had been around in one form or another for several years, and by the 1960 presidential campaign, television would truly become the deciding factor, but in 1952 television made a difference at the Republican convention in Chicago, and for the first time a candidate would introduce to the American voter campaign films (some short, some long).

In 1952, really for the first time, we can see the power of middle-class voters, now in the process of moving from the inner cities out into the more conservative suburbs; organized labor, for the first time, became a significant voting bloc capable of swaying industrial regions of the nation; women became a significant antiwar bloc, who feared sending their sons and husbands into an insignificant war on the other side of the globe; white southerners began making their way slowly into the more conservative Republican Party; and African Americans, just as slowly, began turning their backs on the party of Lincoln.

The election of 1952 was a huge turning point in American political history. New groups were forming, new coalitions were forming, and a new attitude toward the world was beginning to take shape. The political world of today had its beginnings in 1952, an election that seemed to have little significance at the time, mostly because it was a landslide for Eisenhower and few people remember the Democratic nominee Adlai Stevenson. For most Americans, the pendulum had simple swung back, Ike was the obvious leader, and Stevenson (if at all he is remembered) was the candidate with the hole in his shoe. But the 1952 campaign was truly the beginning of modern American politics.

Gary Donaldson
New Orleans

Chapter 1

"Background to the Age, and the Scramble to Nominate Eisenhower"

Just prior to the 1952 presidential election, political scientist James MacGregor Burns suggested that if the Republicans did not win in 1952 that the party might actually cease to exist. The Republicans had been crushed by Roosevelt in four consecutive elections, and then by Truman in 1948. The title of his article was "Is Our Two-Party System in Danger?" His answer, of course, was "no."[1] In his 1956 study, *Revolt of the Moderates*, Samuel Lubell, another prominent political scientist, wrote of American politics at mid-century: "The 1952 election may well have been our most emotional campaign since the McKinley-Bryan or Hoover-Smith contests." He called Dwight Eisenhower's victory a "crucial turn" in American political history and further compared it to Andrew Jackson's victory in 1828, Lincoln's in 1860, and Franklin Roosevelt's victory over Herbert Hoover in 1932.[2] Pollster Lou Harris—in his book *Is There A Republican Majority?*—wrote about the election: "What has happened . . . is that the basic Democratic majority has been broken. But, perhaps more important, the Republicans have put together a permanent majority of their own." There is, he added, "the possibility of a permanent political revolution stemming out of the 1952 election of Dwight Eisenhower."[3] Burns, Harris, and Lubell were all correct. The Republican Party did not wither and die, and the 1952 election was a significant turning point in American political history. Eisenhower's election had changed the political dynamic. His popularity and moderation as a candidate and then as president caused independents and political neophytes to flood into the Republican Party. Although three out of every five Americans continued to call themselves Democrats in 1952, one in four who had voted for Truman in 1948 jumped ship in 1952 and voted for Eisenhower.[4]

Even though Eisenhower was willing to accept many of the old New Deal promises and programs, his election brought an end to the era of New Deal liberalism as a political entity. Eisenhower's election also ended the age of Democratic dominance that had lasted since the early 1930s. The 1952 election established parity again between the two political parties, a parity that had not been seen in the nation's politics for much of the century.

Life had been difficult for the Republicans through the 1930s and the 1940s. Kept out of the presidency since 1933 (and in the minority in Congress since 1931), they had become little more than an opposition party. In addition, they were fiercely divided. The liberals (still often described in the 1940s as progressives) had little in common with the party's Old Guard—the conservatives and isolationists. Roosevelt and the Democrats had made political hay through three national elections (1932, 1936, and 1940) by blaming the Great Depression on the Republicans; and the Republican liberals, had in turn, maintained control in their own party by laying blame for the party's woes on the right-wing conservatives. The result was liberal (really better described in this period as moderates) Republican candidates for president: Alf Landon in 1936 and Wendell Willkie in 1940. To Old Guard conservatives like Ohio Senator Robert Taft, this development was little more that "me-tooism," and it offered little chance of success against Roosevelt and the powerful Democrats.[5]

Not only had the Democrats forced the Republicans to carry the political blame for the Great Depression, but they had also successfully blamed the Republicans for the tremendous foreign policy mistake of isolationism. Several Republican isolationists, mostly from the Midwest, had opposed America's entrance into World War II. Almost immediately following the bombing of Pearl Harbor and America's entrance into the war (both in the Pacific and in Europe), it became apparent that entering the war had been the right thing to do, that Japan and Nazi Germany were obvious evils, and that the effort of the United States was necessary to rid the world of their aggressions. As the war began to draw to a close, the old prewar isolationists in the Republican Party appeared to be from another era, and the image hurt the party at the polls.

But a shift in the political landscape became apparent toward the end of the war. There was a prevailing opinion that the time for Democratic domination was over, that the pendulum was about to swing back and a tsunami of Republicanism was about to wash over Washington. Political pundits also saw that the emergencies that had brought the Democrats to power in the first place were also over. The Great Depression was at an end and that the policies needed to fight that economic disaster were no longer necessary. With the war ending, there was no longer the concern that changing boats in midstream might somehow jeopardize America's war-making capabilities. The time for a Republican Party resurgence had finally come.

As the 1944 campaign approached, Republicans began casting about for a candidate that might be able to unseat Roosevelt and the Democrats. They looked first to General Douglas MacArthur, the theater commander in Asia, a military hero, and an outspoken conservative all his life; and then to General Dwight Eisenhower, the Allied commander in Europe, a military hero of equal or even greater status than MacArthur, but something of a political enigma. It had been suggested to Eisenhower by a war correspondent as early as 1943 that politics might be in his future. The general's only response was that the correspondent had surely "been standing in the sun too long."[6] But by late 1943 and early 1944, the drumbeat quickened as the Republicans became increasingly desperate. Arthur Eisenhower counseled his younger brother to issue a statement immediately that he was not interested in a political career, arguing that MacArthur's military reputation had been damaged because he had refused to step away from the political arena. Dwight Eisenhower responded that any such statement would only make him appear ridiculous, and that he would not, he wrote to his brother, "Tolerate the use of my name in connection with any political activity of any kind."[7] There was even some additional talk that Roosevelt might choose Eisenhower as his running mate in 1944, particularly if the Republicans nominated MacArthur.[8] But both MacArthur and Eisenhower became consumed with the war effort, and all talks of making generals into politicians in the midst of the war quieted.

In 1944 the Republicans went through one more cycle of their Roosevelt-era defeatist plan when they passed over their 1940 candidate, Wendell Willkie, and nominated Thomas E. Dewey, the well-known New York City gangbuster and popular New York State governor—and like Willkie, a moderate. Despite predictions of a Republican victory from the likes of journalist and pundit Walter Lippmann and a Republican endorsement from the powerful United Mine Workers head John L. Lewis, Roosevelt won the election fairly handily (54 to 46 percent), although Dewey had gotten closer to Roosevelt than either of his two Republican predecessors. The 1944 campaign had at least two dramatic events: Roosevelt was persuaded by big-city bosses and Southern conservatives in his party to dump his second vice president, Henry Wallace, and choose instead Missouri Senator Harry S. Truman, a moderate Democrat, a New Dealer, and the popular head of a Senate wartime investigating committee. The choice became known as the "Second Missouri Compromise," and was considered foolhardy by many who thought that there was a good chance that Roosevelt would not live out his fourth term. Then in October, Roosevelt dispelled all rumors about his deteriorating health by campaigning through New York City during a heavy rainstorm with the top down on his limousine.[9]

On February 20, 1945, Vice President Truman heard that Roosevelt had died. He had been in office only four weeks, and the prospect of taking over the presidency was something that clearly frightened him. The news "swept through the corridors and across the floor" of the Senate, Truman recalled in his memoirs. But it was only a rumor. "There had always been baseless rumors about Roosevelt." Then he added, "I did not want to think about the possibility of his death as President." It was no wonder that rumors flew through Washington in the late winter and early spring of 1945. Truman recalled: "I was shocked by his appearance. His eyes were sunken. His magnificent smile was missing from his careworn face. He seemed a spent man. I had a hollow feeling within me."[10]

In March, when Roosevelt returned from the Yalta Conference, he addressed Congress, and many were alarmed to see how old, thin and frail he looked. He spoke while seated in the well of the House, an unprecedented concession to his physical incapacity. He opened his speech by saying, "I hope that you will pardon me for this unusual posture of sitting down during the presentation of what I want to say, but . . . it makes it a lot easier for me not to have to carry about ten pounds of steel around on the bottom of my legs."[11] On March 29, Roosevelt went to Warm Springs, in Georgia, to recuperate from his trip and to prepare for his appearance at the founding conference of the United Nations. On April 12, he died of a massive stroke. He was just sixty-three.

Roosevelt's death changed so many things, but it was in the arena of foreign affairs that things changed the most. Truman had almost no experience in foreign policy, and to make matters worse, FDR had not bothered to keep his vice president informed on international issues, including the Manhattan Project that resulted in the atomic bomb. In fact, all Truman knew of U.S. foreign policy was what he read in the newspapers. Clearly, the new president was not prepared to handle America's foreign affairs in this new and complex period. When he came to office, the battle on Okinawa was still raging in the Pacific, while in Europe, U.S. and Allied armies moved more quickly than expected toward Soviet forces racing into Germany from the east. On April 30, the Soviets entered Berlin and Hitler committed suicide. It was the beginning of a new era.

At the Potsdam Conference in Berlin in late July 1945, Truman (in office for only a few months) and Eisenhower (then serving as the first governor of the American zone of occupied Germany) were bantering about the postwar world when Truman jolted Eisenhower with a suggestion that he might want to consider a future in politics. "General," Truman said, "there is nothing that you may want that I won't try to help you get. That definitely and specifically includes the Presidency in 1948." Eisenhower later recalled his amazement at the offer. "I doubt that any soldier of our country has ever [been] so suddenly struck in his emotional vitals by a President with such an apparently sincere and certainly astounding proposition as this. . . . [T]o have the President suddenly throw this broadside into me left no recourse except to treat it [as] a very splendid joke which I hoped it was. . . . Mr. President." The General replied, "I don't know who will be your opponent for the presidency, but it will not be I."[12]

When Eisenhower returned home after the war, he was asked over and over: Will you run? To an audience in his hometown of Abilene, Kansas, in 1945 he seemed to make it pretty clear. "It is silly to talk about me in politics," he said, "and so for once I'll talk about it, but only to settle this thing once [and] for all. I should like to make this as emphatic as possible. . . . In the strongest language you can command, you can state that I have no political ambitions at all, make it even stronger than that if you can. I'd like to go even further than Sherman in expressing myself on this subject."[13] He could hardly have been any more definitive, but the 1948 campaign was still three years away, and in that time Eisenhower definitely toyed with the possibility of making a run.

* * *

It is a phenomenon of the American political system that (in order to appeal to the largest possible range of voters) a presidential candidate is often bound to select a running mate who carries nearly the opposite appeal. Such was the case in 1944 when Roosevelt chose Harry Truman as his running mate. In many ways, FDR was an unusual American political figure. He was not a man of the people, not at all the type of figure that the nation, generally, looks to elect. He was urbane, urban, patrician-wealthy, a career politician who had risen to political importance in New York as a reformer who had battled the bossism of Tammany Hall. With the Roosevelt family money and name, he had glided through life from the social prominence of Hyde Park, to Groton, Harvard, and on to Columbia Law. He headed to Wall Street, the New York State Legislature, national politics in 1920, and finally to the White House in 1933. In contrast, Truman could be considered the anti-Roosevelt, FDR's exact opposite. Truman's life had been hard. He grew up on the Missouri frontier where opportunities were limited and prospects were bleak. There was no prominent family name, no family wealth, and no marvelous education to carry him through life. He served with some distinction in France during World War I, and returned home to try his hand at business. His small men's clothing store in Kansas City soon failed. He then speculated in oil and mining interests, failing at those as well. At age thirty and struggling to find his place in the world, he turned to politics and found some success at the local level where he seemed destined to stay. But by allying with the Pendergast political machine, a corrupt Kansas City political organization, Truman moved up the political ladder and finally into the U.S. Senate where he made a name for himself as one of the few southerners who stood by Roosevelt and the New Deal.

Truman stepped into the White House just after FDR's death with a convincing 87 percent approval rating, a figure that clearly owed more to his anonymity and expectations than to his popularity. After about a year and a half, by the time of the 1946 congressional elections, his approval ratings had plummeted to a paltry 32 percent. Truman's greatest challenges in office revolved around Reconversion, the process of regulating the postwar economy that was Truman's first real act as president. And he generally stumbled. Taking advice from economists who believed that an immediate removal of price controls would cause either debilitating inflation or depression, or both, Truman left price controls in place for nearly two years after the war ended. At the same time, organized labor pushed at the other end. Generally quiet during the war years in an effort to keep production up, the nation's labor unions went out on strike all over the nation when the war ended. As labor and other production costs increased and prices remained fixed by the federal government, production of consumer goods ground to a halt. To meet the demand, a vibrant black market emerged, embarrassing the government even more. Finally, under pressure from just about every direction, an embattle Truman removed the price controls. It was a popular decision, but the long wait had hurt the president; his first real decision had been wrong.

Truman's handling of these postwar labor strikes brought the labor unions out against him. Certainly, labor had done its part to win the war, but following V-J Day, the American worker was taking home less real income than in the years before the war. In 1941, the average American worker's real wage was just over $28.00 per week. That had risen to $36.72 by 1945. But by the fall of 1946, inflation and a reduction in overtime pay had pulled real wages back to near the 1941 level. The economic pie was expanding, but labor's share had remained the same. Industry leaders, however, argued that they were shackled with Truman's wartime price controls. In addition, they were stuck with the immense cost of retooling, of converting from wartime to peacetime production.[14] Labor and management were on a collision course that would engulf the immediate postwar years. And Truman, caught in the middle, had no real answers. He would be damaged by the events.

The result was nearly inevitable. Through the summer of 1945, the nation experienced 4,600 work stoppages impacting some 5 million workers. Following V-J Day, the situation worsened. In September, 43,000 oil refinery workers went out on strike, cutting off one-third of the nation's oil supply. Six weeks later, the United Auto Workers struck General Motors, idling some 325,000 workers. Then in January, 750,000 steelworkers walked out, followed by 200,000 electrical workers and another 200,000 meatpackers. The nation seemed on the verge of paralysis, and the American people looked to their president for answers. Truman responded as he often did to crises.

He pulled together a blue ribbon committee of representatives from labor and management to find a solution. They had none.[15]

In April 1946, the United Mineworkers went out on strike and the nation's infrastructure ground to a halt. Truman responded by seizing the mines. It was a decisive, even popular decision, but it alienated organized labor whose leaders and rank and file began to see the president as a tool of management. Finally in May, railroad engineers and trainmen struck, which threatened to shut down commerce and industry. Truman responded by asking Congress for emergency powers to bring contempt charges against labor leaders, and then he threatened to draft striking workers into the military. Truman's threats forced labor leaders in the railroad industry to back down and the president basked in his victory. But as the 1946 midterm elections approached, it was clear that organized labor had no friend in the White House.

As Washington geared up for the 1946 election campaign, Truman's approval ratings hovered in the low thirties. Most Americans had come to see him as a sort of caretaker president, someone who would keep things under control in Washington until the Republicans could finally take over the reins of power. In 1946, the Democratic National Committee had so little confidence in Truman that they purchased national radio time and broadcast old Roosevelt speeches rather than send Truman out on the road to campaign for Democratic Party candidates.[16]

* * *

The Republican Party resurgence took a huge step in the 1946 congressional campaigns when the Republicans swept both houses of Congress for the first time since Hoover was in office. On the first day of the new congressional session, Republican members of the 80th Congress arrived on Capitol Hill carrying brooms. They refused to reveal to the press what the brooms symbolized, but to anyone who knew the mind of the GOP in 1946 they intended to sweep away the New Deal.

Perhaps the most important aspect of the 1946 midterm elections was that the Republicans misread its results. They believed they had been handed a mandate for change, that the era of New Deal liberalism had ended, and that they could now dismantle the New Deal programs. *U.S. News* reported that a new cycle in American political history was beginning and that the Republicans could be expected to remain in office for up to sixteen years.[17] *Newsweek* speculated that the New Deal had ended and announced in a headline: "An Era Begins."[18] To the Republican Senate leader, Robert Taft, the Republican mandate was to "cast out a great many chapters of the New Deal, if not the whole book."[19]

The victory also gave the Republicans tremendous overconfidence. No party had ever won the midterm elections and then gone on to lose the White House two years later, and the Republicans began to plan for the eventuality of controlling both houses of Congress and the White House after 1948. Their attitude seemed to be that they could do as they pleased (at least on domestic issues) without having to worry about suffering any repercussions in the coming presidential election. The result was that the Republican-dominated 80th Congress had little concern for compromise or building coalitions outside its own conservative power base. Also, many Republicans were simply content to wait out the two years until one of their own would be elected president, to do nothing until they controlled both branches of government. By 1948, all this overconfidence would turn in Truman's favor.

"The Little Man from Missouri," as Truman was often called, had brought the war to a conclusion in good order, but to most Americans he had done little more than observe the giant American war machine as it did its business of finishing off Germany and Japan. He had made the decision to drop the bomb on Japan, and he was generally praised for that decisive act—and for ending the war as quickly as possible. But even that was perceived by many Americans as little more than carrying out a decision that had already been made by the nation's great war leaders who had gone before him.

As the next cycle of presidential elections approached, the perception of Truman's general lack of leadership abilities caused a splintering in the Democratic Party. Through the 1930s, FDR had cobbled together a fragile coalition of diverse groups that included Southern conservatives, Northern liberals, Western farmers, organized labor, big-city bosses, and minorities and immigrants in Northern cities. It was apparent that Truman simply did not have the qualities necessary to hold these disparate groups together. Without FDR's leadership, parts of this fragile coalition began to break away, each intending to build its own power base and to lead a new party coalition into the next political generation.

The Republicans of the 80th Congress coalesced around Ohio Senator Robert Taft, "Mr. Republican," the austere conservative and prewar isolationist, the son of a president. Taft, it was no secret, had his eye on the 1948 Republican nomination, and just about everyone agreed that whoever received that nomination would ride the Republican wave into the White House with little difficulty.

Truman and the 80th Congress maintained a unique relationship in postwar politics. On domestic issues, it was a gloves-off affair. The president vetoed seventy-five bills in the two sessions. Five of his vetoes were overridden and very little was accomplished. On foreign affairs, however, it was a different story. The two parties worked together to establish a Cold War foreign policy that would prevail for another forty years. In the final analysis, however,

Truman used the 80th Congress to enhance his standing with several sectors of his party. By introducing and pushing liberal legislation that he almost certainly knew would not pass the conservative 80th Congress, Truman was able to accuse the Republican-dominated Congress of being the political arm of big business, insensitive to the needs of the average American, and unwilling to act on much needed domestic reforms. Consequently, as the 1948 campaign approached, Truman was able to portray himself as the defender of the common man, a fighter against oppression, and the real successor to the New Deal. Then, by opposing the Republican-sponsored Taft-Hartley Act (called the "slave labor bill" by organized labor) Truman was able to pull many of those disgruntled organized labor leaders back into his coalition. On foreign affairs, he worked with congressional leaders to adopt a firm and decisive anti-Soviet stance that was generally popular with the American people. Using Congress as his foil, Truman, by the summer of 1948, had established himself as the new leader of the old New Deal coalition, the defender of the common man and organized labor, and a strong world leader.

In turn, the Republicans in the 80th Congress proceeded under the assumption that the 1946 election was a portent for the future, and that in 1948 they would put one of their own in the White House. That is, they played right into Truman's hands. A Republican bill to reduce taxes in the upper income brackets was passed over Truman's veto. The Republicans excluded several groups from Social Security benefits, overriding two presidential vetoes to get the job done. They killed administration-supported bills to provide aid to education, increase the minimum wage, and provide comprehensive housing. Southern Democrats, seeing no need to support what appeared to be Truman's failing lame-duck presidency, got behind most Republican initiatives in exchange for Republican support in killing civil rights legislation. All this appeared to be an insurmountable obstacle to Truman's domestic agenda, but it worked to increase the president's image with the American people as their representative fighting against the forces of big business and privilege.

After 1946, Taft emerged as the clear leader of the Republicans in Congress, and in that position he was considered the immediate frontrunner for the 1948 Republican nomination. But he was not uncontested. Standing in the wings were at least two formidable candidates: Eisenhower, who continued to claim that politics was not in his future, and Thomas Dewey, who had lost to Roosevelt in 1944 and (it seemed to be common knowledge) would at some point make a run for the 1948 nomination.

Eisenhower was, however, the true wildcard. It was clear that if he wanted the nomination—of either party—he could have it. And that was, in fact, part of his appeal. He wanted to be all things to all people, and that made him a sort of apolitical figure. Few knew if he was a Republican or a Democrat, and he refused to reveal his position, even to the point of avoiding issues that might define him. In this noncandidate roll, he was able to maintain a candidate's visibility without carrying the weight of a candidate's responsibilities. With his intentions unknown, no one dared attack him, and he made no enemies. Nor was he responsible to the press or the public for possessing policies on specific issues. All of this added to his growing popularity. In a 1947 poll, 22 percent believed Eisenhower was a Republican; 20 percent thought he was a Democrat. The largest group, 58 percent, confessed that they did not know his affiliation. In 1946, *Time* reported the obvious: he had what it took to run successfully on either ticket.[20]

The boom for Ike began immediately following the Republican 1946 victory when it seemed clear that the Republican tide was on the rise. *Time* referred to his "tremendous reputation, unencumbered by political liabilities, his wonderful name, his poise, and amazing popularity. . . . Ike," the article continued, "might find it hard to slap down the presidential bee." *Life* reported that Eisenhower was on the stump, despite his almost constant insistence that he was not a candidate, and discussing various issues beyond the military, "thereby starting a big boom to make him a presidential candidate." Another *Life* article announced that a "boom for Ike" was underway and included a cover shot of a pretty girl wearing a "Draft Ike" button as a monocle.[21]

Despite Eisenhower's statements that he had no interest in politics, he clearly wanted to be in the public eye. Between the end of the war and the 1948 election, he gave over 120 formal addresses, and was probably the most sought-after speaker in the nation after the president. He spoke beyond political issues, focusing mostly on peace, patriotism, unity, and the virtues of freedom. Consequently, he looked and talked like a candidate with the important exception that he refrained from political attacks. In a time when the nation was ready to put behind itself the fifteen years of Democratic-sponsored crusades and return to some semblance of normalcy, Eisenhower was a voice of moderation and calm.

Eisenhower continued to deny his candidacy. Finally, in June 1947, he announced that he had agreed to become the president of Columbia University in New York. There, he told a friend, he would find "some shelter from the constant political darts that are launched in my direction by well-meaning, but I fear short sighted, friends."[22] That might have been a logical conclusion, but the nation's politicos saw it differently. Some saw his Columbia position as an affirmation that he wanted to remain in the public eye and in public service. Journalist John Gunther wrote that Eisenhower's announcement that he would go to Columbia caused "the movement to make him President to spread like fire through dry wheat."[23]

In late 1947 Eisenhower did not want to run, but he continued to toy with the possibility. To his friend and wartime chief of staff, Walter Bedell Smith, he wrote: "I do not believe that you or I or anyone else has the right to state categorically that he will *not* perform *any* duty that his country might demand of him." To refuse to run, he told Smith, "would be almost the same thing as a soldier refusing to carry out the desires of his commander." He added that he had no taste for political life, but perhaps under the right circumstances he might reconsider. "On the other hand, if you should assume the occurrence of an American miracle of a nature that has never heretofore occurred, at least since Washington, you might have the spectacle of someone being named by common consent."[24] Eisenhower often referred to his fantasy of being drafted by acclamation. To another friend he wrote: "Since no man—at least since Washington's day—has ever gone into high political office except with his own consent, indeed with his own connivance, I feel perfectly secure in my position" of rejecting a candidacy.[25]

His decision not to run became clearer as he considered other factors. He had come to believe that politicians were only interested in him as a candidate because of his status as a war hero, that his only real virtue was that he was popular enough to win the presidency. It was never in Eisenhower's nature to be an ineffectual front man for a political organization—and the idea was repugnant to him. He told his brother Milton that he did not feel any sense of duty toward a political party that would, "in desperation, turn to some name that might be a bit popular around the country, in the effort to drag a political . . . organization out of a hole."[26] And then there were the rigors of the campaign itself. If he chose to run in 1948 as a Republican, he would have to fight several primary battles, and since primary victories garnered less than half the delegates needed to win the nomination, he would almost certainly be forced into a bloody convention fight as well. Eisenhower may have been a popular national figure, but it would take a great deal to win a party's nomination in 1948. Convention delegates would be hard to come by in a political system that still chose delegates mostly through state legislative caucuses and pandered to political insiders and the wishes of local political machines. Of course, he would not be running unopposed. Taft and Dewey were not likely to give up without a struggle, and their combined forces might well push Eisenhower right out of the arena. He also had no real political organization, and he had raised no money. Rather than risk his reputation in a bloody battle that he might well lose, Eisenhower would decline.

No doubt it was a difficult decision. He probably realized that 1948 might well be his last chance to make a run. Like everyone else in 1947, he certainly saw that the Republicans would take the White House the next year, and (baring major mistakes) probably hold it for two terms. His next chance to run, he probably thought, would not be until 1956. At age sixty-six, he most likely expected to have retired from public service by then, living quietly somewhere, content in having done his duty for his nation.

Eisenhower's hand was finally forced in January 1948 when a group of his supporters entered his name in the March New Hampshire primary. Either he had to allow it to happen and be a candidate or had to publicly withdraw. The intentions of these Eisenhower supporters were apparently not known to Eisenhower until Leonard Finder, the publisher of the Manchester *Union Leader*, sent him a copy of the newspaper's endorsement. Along with the column, Finder added a personal note designed to appeal to what many believed was Eisenhower's desire for a draft: "While we appreciate that you are not anxious for political aspirations, we are equally confident that you will not resist or resent a genuine grass-roots movement. That is exactly what we have here in New Hampshire." In a reference to Eisenhower's long-held commitment to duty, Finder concluded, "No man should deny the will of the people in a matter such as this. All that we are attempting is to have the will of the people made so clear that it cannot be obviated by the usual politicians assembled in convention."[27]

Eisenhower had to respond. He immediately issued a statement claiming that he had no desire to enter politics. Nine days later, on January 23, he issued a more formal response in a letter to Finder that was released to the press.[28] It was as close to Sherman's statement as Eisenhower would get. He wrote that he was not surprised that admirers and supporters had misinterpreted or found hidden meaning in his statements, "but my failure to convince thoughtful and earnest men . . . proves that I must make some amplification. I am not available and could not accept nomination to high political office." He went on to apologize to those who had given their time on his behalf. He concluded with a statement that should have left nothing to the imagination: "My decision to remove myself completely from the political scene is definite and positive [and] I could not accept nomination even under the remote circumstances that it were tendered me."[29] That, he thought, would certainly end all the speculation. He wrote to a friend, "I feel as if I've had an abscessed tooth pulled."[30] And with that, the Republicans stood down and began looking for other candidates. For the Democrats, however, it was a different story. They seemed to interpret Eisenhower's response to Finder's letter as a disavowal of his Republican affiliation. Thus, they concluded, he must be a Democrat.

Like the Republicans, the Democrats had been trying for some time to persuade Eisenhower to cast his lot with them, and he had refused just as he had refused the Republicans. But the Democrats were more desperate in 1948 than the Republicans. They believed that Truman could not win, and they saw no one on the horizon except Eisenhower who had enough popular support to unseat Truman at the convention and then defeat the Republican candidate in November. The objective of these Democrats-for-Eisenhower was little more than to keep the Democrats in Washington (and the Republicans out) for another four years. When Ike wrote to Milton in October 1947 about a political party that "in desperation [would] turn to some name that might be a bit popular around the country, in the effort to drag [itself] out of a hole," he no doubt had the Democrats in mind. At the same time, the Democrats were not just infatuated with Eisenhower, they knew the situation well. Polls showed that Eisenhower-as-Democrat running against any Republican was a winner in 1948.[31]

The draft-Eisenhower Democrats were a fairly diverse group, ranging from the sons of Franklin Roosevelt to labor leaders like Walter Reuther and big-city bosses like Chicago's Jacob Arvey and Jersey City's Frank Hague. There were even Southern supporters, particularly Alabama Senators Lister Hill and John Sparkman, and Florida Senator Claude Pepper. Their only real common cause was that they could not stomach the doomed Truman, and they wanted to keep the Democrats in power. The real force behind the movement, however, was the Americans for Democratic Action (ADA), a liberal political organization that considered itself the harbinger of New Deal liberalism (they called themselves progressives) that, at the same time, despised communism both at home and abroad. To the ADA, 1948 politics was defined as "anyone but Truman." Their political philosophy in 1948 was summed up in a letter from theologian and ADA founder Reinhold Niebuhr to ADA head James Loeb: "We are sunk now" with Truman, he wrote, "and Eisenhower is the only possible candidate who [can] defeat the Republicans. I would support almost any decent man to avoid four years of Republican rule."[32]

In mid-April, 1948, the executive board of the ADA met to devise a strategy to organize the diverse Eisenhower supporters under ADA leadership. They issued a statement designed to pull directly on the strings of Eisenhower's sense of responsibility to the nation: "This Nation has the right to call upon men like Dwight D. Eisenhower . . . if the people so chose. . . . No one . . . can enjoy the privilege of declaring himself unavailable in this hour of the nation's need." Eisenhower, he added, "would stir the popular enthusiasm which will sweep progressive candidates across the country into Congress."[33] For the ADA, the Eisenhower drive was an expedient, an act of desperation. He was simply someone the ADA and other Democrats thought could win—and defeat the others.

Eisenhower had managed to keep his distance from much of this Democratic Party activity as it developed during the early spring of 1948. By March, however, local Democratic Eisenhower-for-president organizations had begun to spring up throughout the country and many were raising money to support the Eisenhower campaign that did not exist. By April, Eisenhower realized that he would again have to deny all charges that he wanted to be a candidate—this time for the benefit of the Democrats. On the day following the ADA endorsement, Eisenhower wrote Bedell Smith, "Recently the Democrats have taken the attitude that Mr. Truman cannot be re-elected;

therefore they do not want to re-nominate him. In this situation they are turning desperately to anyone that might give them a chance of winning, and they have the cockeyed notion that I might be tempted to make the effort."[34]

The ADA endorsement was reported in *Time* on April 19. In that same issue, Eisenhower was asked to respond. "I wrote a letter," he said, referring to the Finder Letter of some four months earlier. "And I meant every word of it."[35] But even that did not satisfy some Democrats. Claude Pepper and other Democrats continued to push for an Eisenhower nomination. In the weeks before the Democratic convention, James Roosevelt sent telegrams to each party delegate inviting them to a meeting to select "the ablest and strongest man available. . . . It is our belief," the message continued, "that no man in these critical days can refuse the call to duty and leadership implicit in the nomination and virtual election to the Presidency of the United States."[36] And again, Eisenhower's hand was forced. On July 5, he issued a statement: "I will not, at this time, identify myself with any political party, and could not accept nomination for any public office or participate in partisan political contest."[37] But because Eisenhower had used the phrase, "at this time," the fires continued to burn. A plan was hatched to have Eisenhower's name placed in nomination at the convention without his consent. Claude Pepper sent a note to Eisenhower notifying him of the plan, and then he concluded the note with: "I neither expect nor desire either an acknowledgment or reply."[38] The scheme forced Eisenhower to disavow his political ambitions one more time. On July 8 and 9, Eisenhower wrote letters to the leaders of the draft-Eisenhower movement. All the letters were personalized and written differently, but each letter contained the following phrase: "No matter under what terms, conditions, or premises a proposal might be couched, I would refuse to accept the nomination."[39] And with that, the 1948 draft-Eisenhower movement was finally shut down.

The Republicans went on, for a second time, to choose Thomas Dewey after Dewey jumped into several primaries in the eleventh hour and then outmaneuvered Taft at the convention to win the nomination. To just about anyone paying attention in 1948, Dewey was about to become the next president. Since there seemed to be no battle to win, he followed the advice of those around him and hardly bothered to campaign; and as the election approached, he leaked his cabinet choices.

The Democrats split badly. Henry Wallace took a challenge from party liberals and formed a third party: the Progressives. Many of the Southern conservatives had become disenchanted with Truman and his concessions toward civil rights for African Americans, and at the convention they walked out. Eventually these neo-secessionists formed the States Rights Democrats, a name quickly whittled down to the Dixiecrats by Southern newspaper editors. Their claim—as it had been the claim of southerners through the nation's history—was that they represented the true aspirations and beliefs of the Democratic Party; that it was the national party that had varied from the party's mainstream structure. They nominated South Carolina Governor Strom Thurmond for president.

In the final analysis, to just about everyone's surprise, Truman won the election fairly easily, carrying 49.5 percent of the popular vote to Dewey's 45 percent. The Electoral College vote was even more convincing with Truman winning a solid 303 votes to Dewey's 189.

Thurmond won thirty-nine electoral votes in four Southern states, but his most important impact was to carry the racist label. That, along with the president's concessions to civil right, gave Truman a big turnout of African American voters in Northern urban areas. He may have lost thirty-nine electoral votes in South Carolina, Louisiana, Alabama, and Mississippi, but he won California, Illinois, and Ohio (at least in part) because African American voters there turned out in big numbers in Los Angeles, Chicago, and Cleveland. It was a good tradeoff for Truman, and it began a shift in the national party structure as conservative white southerners began moving into the Republican Party and Northern blacks began deserting the party of Lincoln for the Democrats.

Wallace's impact was much the same. Republicans had wanted desperately to label Truman a Communist, or at least soft on communism. But Wallace had, almost eagerly, accepted support and assistance from the American Communist Party in his campaign. Any attempt to attack Truman as a Communist sympathizer fell on deaf ears with Wallace in the race. Although Thurmond's campaign from the Right and Wallace's campaign from the Left may have actually split the Democrats, both of those third-party efforts aided Truman's campaign by deflecting criticisms that might well have damaged Truman. Because of Thurmond and Wallace, the volatile charges of racism and communism did not stick to Truman.[40]

The Republican defeat was a devastating blow. Republicans had come to believe, through the two decades of Democratic Party dominance, that they could not win because of what Samuel Lubell called that "devilishly clever FDR."[41] Then they were beaten by the hapless Truman. Republican leaders allowed themselves to believe that they had lost in 1948 because no one went to the polls, and that the pollsters had predicted such a large Republican landslide that many Americans simply decided that Dewey's election was a foregone conclusion and they decided not to participate. But, as Lubell points out, more former FDR supporters stayed away from the polls in 1948 than Republicans.[42] A few pundits even began to consider the death of the Republican Party and the demise of the two-party system.[43] But within two years, the Republicans had already begun another resurgence, winning twenty-eight seats in the House and five in the Senate in the 1950 congressional elections.

It seemed to show that Truman's popularity in 1948 was little more than a flash in the pan, a political perfect storm that favored Truman at one political moment in history. Before the 1948 election, Truman's approval ratings were dismal. By November 1950, they had returned to their low levels. Voters were again looking toward a new era of Republican domination in Washington and the election of 1952.

Chapter 2

Stevenson of Illinois

As the 1948 presidential campaign approached, two of the most important political figures in the Illinois Democratic Party had jumped on the abortive draft-Eisenhower bandwagon: Cook County political boss Jacob Arvey, and the state party's chosen candidate for the Senate seat that year, Paul Douglas. Adlai Stevenson, the Democratic Party's choice to run for governor against two-time Republican incumbent Dwight Green, had refused to join the Eisenhower movement and stood by Truman. Then at the convention, once the draft-Eisenhower movement had collapsed, Stevenson seconded the nomination of his distant cousin (and Truman's good friend) Alben Barkley for vice president.

As late as the last weeks of October, just before the election, *The New York Times* followed most political pundits and predicted that Green would defeat Stevenson by a wide margin. Most pollsters had by then given up the polling process, declaring Dewey's victory a foregone conclusion—along with most of the other Republicans who expected to ride his coattails into Washington. Green was so overconfident, in fact, that he spent much of the summer lobbying for the vice presidential nomination instead of campaigning for the job in Springfield. He was then considered a contender for the number-two spot on the ticket, and he was chosen to deliver the keynote address at the Republican National Convention in Philadelphia. He was, however, too far to the right for what Dewey needed in a running mate, and he was finally overlooked in favor of California Governor Earl Warren, a moderate.

When the Illinois election-night numbers rolled in, it was clear that Stevenson had made a considerable difference. He buried Green with a whopping 57 percent of the votes, the largest plurality in the state's history. His margin of victory was almost 600,000 votes, and he took half of the traditionally conservative downstate counties. Truman won the state by a squeak of just 33,000 votes—in fact, riding Stevenson's coattails to victory. Illinois was a crucial state and a big win. Although Truman and Stevenson had very little in common and really never connected on any level, Truman would never forget Stevenson's loyalty and his role in the 1948 election. In 1952, when Truman began looking around for a successor, Stevenson, one of the party's fresh faces, would make the short list.[1]

Stevenson was one of several Democrats who emerged with victories in 1948, along with Hubert Humphrey and Lyndon Johnson. John Kennedy, another fresh-faced Democrat, won a second term in the House.[2] Although Kennedy had served in the war, and emerged as something of a war hero, Stevenson had more administrative and political experience than Kennedy. During the war, Stevenson had served in the Navy Department as the assistant to Secretary Frank Knox, and he was sent on several inspection tours of naval installations in the Pacific. As early as 1942, Stevenson, at the young age of forty-two, considered a run for the Senate from Illinois against Republican Curly Brooks, but the all-powerful Chicago Democratic Party machine overlooked Stevenson in favor of Congressman Raymond McKeough.[3]

Stevenson then turned his interests toward the state gubernatorial election in 1944. But as the campaign approached, he simply could not make the decision to run, and that indecision exposed what some have considered a serious flaw in Stevenson's character. Stevenson's indecisiveness was almost legendary in a profession where the ability to make quick and decisive decisions is considered an attribute. Several times, including his decision to run in 1952, Stevenson seemed almost debilitated by apprehension, much to the frustration of his supporters. His friends and cohorts have often argued that it was not so much indecision that plagued Stevenson, as a natural lack of desire to promote himself, and a central belief that the office should seek the individual rather that the other way around. He was also careful and cautious about such decisions. Nevertheless, the image stuck like glue to Stevenson throughout his political career. He was always portrayed as an indecisive figure who might not be up to the job when the tough decisions had to be made. That often translated into what one of his biographers referred to as a "soft head," a leader who begs off toughness for a compromising and conciliatory approach. As a presidential candidate during the first decade of the Cold War, such an image was not helpful.[4]

Stevenson, however, was burdened with more than just the decision to run. His wife, Ellen, hated Washington, and in 1943, she returned to the Stevenson family home in Libertyville, Illinois. There have been hints that Adlai may have been unfaithful to their marriage in this period, perhaps in response to Ellen's unmanageable mental illness. As early as 1941 Ellen asked for a divorce, and the couple's marriage problems continued to escalate through Stevenson's 1948 gubernatorial campaign. In 1949 the couple ended their marriage.[5] Stevenson was also distracted by his attempt to buy the *Chicago Daily News*. Apparently also affecting his decision to run was his belief that the Democratic era was at a close and that a new Republican age would probably have no place for him. He seemed to be torn between conflicting desires to be an attorney in Chicago, a politician, a diplomat, or a newspaper man. But with the agony building up in his marriage, it is a small wonder that the decision to run for governor in 1944 was a difficult one. He finally demurred.

When Frank Knox died, somewhat unexpectedly in April 1944, Stevenson began his abortive attempt to buy the *Chicago Daily News* (which had been published by Knox until 1940). But within the year, that project had collapsed and Stevenson had been eased out of the Navy Department, now under the leadership of James Forrestal, who saw Stevenson as too conciliatory—too soft for the position.[6] From there, Stevenson went on to the State Department to become part of the U.S. commission to establish the United Nations. Serving mostly under Archibald MacLeish, Stevenson became the senior advisor to the nation's U.N. delegation and was named an alternate delegate in the fall of 1946. He also represented the Truman administration on a number of committees.[7]

In November 1946, Stevenson's assumptions and fears about the changing winds of national politics seemed to come true when the Republicans swept the nation in the midterm elections, capturing both houses of Congress for the first time since 1931. It seemed to be the wave of the future. In Illinois, Democrats held on to only six of the state's twenty-six congressional seats, and even most of the party machine candidates in Chicago were turned out. There was, however, one bright spot for the Democrats that seemed to awaken Stevenson. In the spring of 1947, Martin Kennelly was elected mayor of Chicago. An honest, civic-minded, Democrat, Kennelly changed the face of Chicago-Cook County Democratic Party politics from the besmirched organization led by political bosses Ed Kelly and Jake Arvey to a new appearance of honesty and good government. Stevenson seemed to take from Kennelly's victory that there was still a place in government for honesty and moderation. Stevenson wrote to a friend, "Kennelly's victory has reinvigorated the local [Democrats] and suggested the revolutionary idea that you can do better with good candidates."[8] Stevenson fit that bill—as a moderate, reliable, good-government Democrat.

Although Stevenson was the central figure of American postwar liberalism, it is difficult to categorize him as a true New Deal-style liberal. He was not, in fact, the liberal that most American liberals expected him to be. Part of his appeal may have been his willingness to attack the Republicans at a time when the rise of the Republican Right, for many Democrats, meant a need to find some accommodation with the new political order. While Democratic leaders (particularly Southern leaders like Georgia Senator Richard

Russell, Texas Senator Lyndon Johnson, and House Democratic Leader Sam Rayburn, also from Texas) tried to work with Republican moderates, Stevenson often attacked Republicans as aloof, isolationist, and narrowly nationalistic. He was also an ardent internationalist and antifascist in the prewar years, standing against the popular isolationism of other Midwestern politicians like Taft. In the early 1950s, he often and aggressively confronted the anti-Communist hysteria of the era and refused to back down in the face of right-wing Republican attacks. That alone brought many of the nation's liberals to his side. Stevenson also fit the liberal bill as an intellectual—or at least he gave the appearance of being one. Most liberals had seen FDR as an intellectual, mostly because he sounded like one, and he was willing to accept and implement new ideas. Liberals wanted Stevenson to capture that image again. If he was not intellectual, his oratorical style seemed to perk the ears of many liberals because in some ways that was like their beloved Roosevelt, particularly in the way he delivered speeches. He was eloquent, quick, and sharp-witted. He was also often described as charming—words used to describe Roosevelt.[9]

Stevenson was, however, a fairly conservative patrician attorney, an elitist who spent most of his political life courting downstate Illinois conservatives and independents, and well outside most liberal circles. According to George Ball, one of Stevenson's closest advisors, Stevenson was "never a real liberal."[10] And John Kenneth Galbraith once said of Stevenson that "he ran for President not to rescue the downtrodden but to resume the responsibilities properly belonging to the privileged."[11] In that way he may well have been much like Roosevelt.

For the nation's liberals, one of the most troubling aspects of Stevenson's political life was his refusal to join the ADA. ADA leaders like Walter Reuther, Hubert Humphrey, James Carey, Eleanor Roosevelt, and ADA chairman James Loeb would one day be Stevenson's most ardent supporters, but when the ADA was forming in the years right after the war, Stevenson refused to attend its organizational meeting, or even address ADA dinners. Almost certainly Stevenson saw the ADA as too radical for his blood and possibly detrimental to his future as a politician.[12] In 1952, in an outburst that must have caused the ADA leadership to wince, Stevenson said that "I don't agree with your program." He added that he did not see eye to eye with the ADA's support of public housing, had no interest in repealing Taft-Hartley, did not support federal aid to education, and disliked what he called "socialized medicine." He added that he believed that civil rights was the concern of the states and not the federal government, and that he had no intention of putting "the South completely over a barrel" over the issue. "You know," he continued, "I've got southern blood in me."[13] On the economy, he took his most conservative stance by insisting that he could not abide the rising national debt. In a speech in early 1950, he warned that "beneath the heavy hand" of "the monster state . . . the only thing worse than neglect and too little government is paternalism and too much government."[14] Carl McGowan, a close associate of Stevenson, recalled in the years following Stevenson's two presidential campaigns that "those who said they were for Eisenhower solely for reasons of fiscal responsibility knew not whereof they spoke. They voted against the man who was . . . their dream candidate."[15]

Stevenson, in fact, may have been more in tune politically with the early twentieth-century progressives than with the mid-century liberals—he may have had more in common with Theodore Roosevelt than with Teddy's cousin Franklin. Like the progressives, he saw government (both state and federal) as the nation's moral center, both efficient and honest. As Illinois governor, he went a long way toward cleaning up the corruption in the state government and ending the influence of the successors to Al Capone's crime syndicate. He defended states' rights because he believed, like the progressives, that state governments could serve as laboratories of social experimentation while solving local social problems. At the same time, he fought for a state-controlled Federal Employment Practices Commission (FEPC) that would encourage minority hiring for state jobs, although the Illinois State Legislature refused to support it. He thought that the nation's budget should be balanced, and he did not believe in the gross expansion of federal powers. "If we can't balance our national budget now, when will we," Stevenson asked a crowd of Democrats in early 1950. "And I hope and pray that history will never record that the Democratic Party foundered on the rocks of fiscal responsibility after leading America boldly, wisely, [and] courageously, through two world wars and the most extensive social revolution in the short period of time in history."[16] All of this does not mean that Stevenson was, necessarily, out of step with national politics in postwar America, but for most liberals a call for a balance budget was cut from the cloth of conservative economic policy.

Stevenson's willingness to stand up to Joseph McCarthy and the Red Scare of the early 1950s, when others would not, may well have endeared him to the Left more than anything else. In 1951, Stevenson, as governor of Illinois, had vetoed the Broyles bill. Often called the "Little McCarthy" bill, the Broyles bill would have made it a felony in Illinois to belong to a subversive group, and required a loyalty oath of all public employees and candidates for office in Illinois. While much of the political world was cowering before McCarthy's perceived power, Stevenson took a stand against his excesses.

Stevenson had a brush with communism that would haunt his 1952 campaign. Richard Nixon had become one of the nation's most important figures in the war against communism. In 1948, California Congressman Nixon, then a member of the House Committee on Un-American Activities (HUAC), broke the spy case against Alger Hiss, a high-ranking State Department official who most believed was on track to one day be secretary of state. In August 1948, Whitaker Chambers, an editor at *Time*, claimed that in the 1930s he had been a secret courier for the Communist Party. He then accused Hiss of being one of his accomplices. Most who dealt with the case thought Chambers (whose Communist background alone caused his reputation to be suspect) had fabricated the story. But Nixon believed Chambers, and he pushed hard in an attempt to convict Hiss. Nixon managed to produce some microfilm hidden in a pumpkin that seemed to point to Hiss's guilt. Hiss denied the charges and was indicted by a federal grand jury on two counts of perjury. To American liberals, the case became something of a cause célèbre at least in part because Hiss was a darling of the liberals, and because Nixon and others on the Republican Right had begun to use the case to attack other liberals who had been associated with Hiss. Hiss's attorneys had hoped to exonerate their client by parading a series of witnesses before the grand jury to testify to Hiss's good character. In that capacity, Stevenson was asked to testify. Stevenson and Hiss had been little more than acquaintances when both worked at the Agricultural Adjustment Administration in the 1930s.[17]

At first, Stevenson refused to testify, citing the burden of his work in Springfield. But he finally agreed to give a deposition under oath. He explained that he had known Hiss only briefly, and when asked if he could testify to the level of Hiss's integrity, loyalty, and veracity, Stevenson responded "good."[18] The testimony, as insignificant as it was, was used against Stevenson throughout the 1952 campaign, and then for the remainder of his political career as an example of his "soft" stance on communism. But to American liberals, it made Stevenson the very pillar of integrity when many in the political and entertainment worlds were denouncing others to save their own skins and careers.

The entire incident made Nixon something of a hero among his party's right wing, and as Eisenhower began to move toward the Republican nomination, it was Nixon (the Communist hunter and right-wing hero) who moved to the front of the line as the nominee's possible running mate.

Stevenson also attacked McCarthyism. In June, 1950 he told a group of supporters in Chicago:

> We are behaving like nutty neurotics. We . . . are nervously looking for subversive enemies under the bed and behind the curtains. We exchange frenzied, irresponsible accusations of disloyalty. 'Guilt by association' has been added to our language. The slander is honored. The shadow of a nameless fear slopes across the land. There is talk of thought control among Jefferson's people.[19]

A year later, during a commencement address at the University of Illinois, he lashed out at McCarthyism, calling it a "hysterical form of putrid slander."[20]

Neither the Broyles bill veto nor Stevenson's testimony in the Hiss case can be counted as powerful stances against McCarthyism or the Red Scare.

Stevenson's message in vetoing the Broyles bill was based mostly on his belief that the bill would be ineffective in stopping the spread of communism. He wrote, "Does anyone seriously think that a real traitor will hesitate to sign a loyalty oath?"[21] And the Hiss deposition was little more than a statement of recollection about a man he had known only casually. But together, for American liberals looking for a standard bearer, they made Stevenson a champion in the face of America's growing anti-Communist movement. He would continue to be their man.

Stevenson, like most Americans, had formed his foreign policy opinions from the lessons of World War II and the developing postwar conflict with the Soviets. During the war, he seemed to hold hope, as did many in government, including the president, that the end of World War II would bring a healthy relationship between the United States and the Soviet Union. When the war ended, Stevenson began his tenure as a U.S. representative at the U.N. organizational meetings in San Francisco. From there, he quickly saw that the Americans and the Soviets were headed down a pathway of distrust and power politics, and he hoped that the United States would work to avoid alienating and isolating Moscow. Unlike George Kennan and others at the Pentagon, Stevenson refused to concede that the Soviets were innately expansionist, arguing instead that if Joseph Stalin and the Moscow leadership were allowed to develop what they considered a satisfactory level of security, and then be convinced of the West's peaceful intentions, that any impending East-West conflict could be avoided. He expressed, for instance, a fear that a combination of Western nations might continually out vote the Soviets in the U.N. General Assembly resulting in an isolated, cornered and eventually combative Moscow.[22]

But like most diplomats in this period, much of Stevenson's optimism faded as the Cold War hardened into a clash over both conflicting economic systems and ideas at various hot and cold points throughout the world. By early 1947, his voice began to harmonize with much of the rest of the West's diplomatic leadership, and he started calling for the containment of Soviet power. As Truman hardened his stance, Stevenson followed. He decried any appeasement of Soviet aggressions and threw his support to the two pillars of containment, the Truman Doctrine and the Marshall Plan.[23] Stevenson soon became to the Democratic Party what John Foster Dulles was to the Republicans: their leader on most foreign policy issues.

Stevenson's one-term tenure as Illinois governor revealed mostly a marked fiscal conservatism combined with a strong reformist tendency. His most liberal initiatives, a constitutional convention to rewrite Illinois's antiquated constitution and a state FEPC, both died at the hands of a hostile state legislature. He did, however, pass labor legislation that increased workman's compensation and unemployment compensation and increased cost-of-living payments for old-age pensioners and the blind. Most of his political failures came from his unwillingness to be a Lyndon Johnson-style compromiser; he too often held his ground and then lost the bill. As his biographer, John Bartlow Martin has written, "His record of legislative achievement was neither really outstanding nor really poor."[24]

In 1951, a series of scandals rocked Stevenson's administration while threatening to blemish his good-government reputation. A Stevenson aide got involved in a gambling-stock deal that was precipitated by the old Capone gang. In July, it was found that a Stevenson appointee in the Illinois Department of Agriculture had allowed horsemeat to be ground in with hamburger in exchange for kickbacks. The ever-hostile *Chicago Tribune* began referring to "Adlaiburgers."[25] Stevenson weathered the Illinois scandals, and they did not filter into his 1952 national campaign, but several of his friends and political acquaintances insisted that the events of the summer of 1951 continued to bother him throughout much of his life.[26]

Democrats, it seems, are always looking for the next new thing, the fresh face to nominate for president. William Jennings Bryan may well have been the first. Even Franklin Roosevelt, out of political view for nearly a decade to recover from polio, re-emerged as a fresh face in 1928, and then as a presidential candidate four years later. Republicans have a tendency to nominate the next in line, the political figure who has paid his dues and worked hardest for the party. Adlai Stevenson was no Franklin Roosevelt. But American liberals found in him an appeal that harkened back to their beloved FDR. It may have been wishful thinking. It may have been hope for the future of their party. It may only have been a fleeting belief that Stevenson, if he won the 1952 election, would be influenced by the liberal forces around him. To American liberals, however, Stevenson looked like a liberal; he acted like a liberal; certainly he talked like a liberal. He probably even walked like a liberal. Their answer was clear. We'll take him.

Chapter 3

Eisenhower Decides to Run

Following Germany's official surrender in the spring of 1945, Eisenhower was appointed military governor of the U.S. occupation zone in Germany, with his offices in Frankfort. In this period he is probably best known for his efforts to change the worldview of the German people from wartime enemies to the victims of Nazism. In November, he was called back to Washington by President Truman to replace his mentor, George Marshall, as chief of staff of the Army. Truman sent Marshall off to China in an ill-fated attempt to broker a peace deal between the Nationalists and the Chinese Communists. In 1948, Eisenhower took his seat as president of Columbia University. From there he fended off the last vestiges of the 1948 Draft-Eisenhower movement. By some accounts, he intended to enjoy a quiet life in academia, write his memoirs, and retire. But within six months, he had become the informal chairman of the Joint Chiefs of Staff, shuttling between the Columbia University campus in New York and the Pentagon in Washington. Then in December 1950, Truman named him the supreme commander of NATO (the North Atlantic Treaty Organization). The next year, Eisenhower's headquarters were designated as the Supreme Headquarters Allied Powers in Europe (SHAPE), and Eisenhower was named the first Supreme Allied Commander Europe (SACEUR) with his headquarters at the Astoria Hotel in central Paris. He continued in that role for about eighteen months, until the summer of 1952, when he returned to the United States to run for president.

Before Eisenhower left for his European command, he chose to clear up a problem. Taft, the Republican frontrunner for the 1952 campaign, had voted against the NATO treaty and then made it clear that he opposed U.S. involvement in any type of collective security. Eisenhower was steeped in internationalism, the belief that an America fully engaged in world events was more of a military deterrent than the isolationism of the prewar years. He believed strongly in NATO, the United Nations, and collective security against international communism. So, before he left for Europe, Eisenhower decided to meet with Taft, get his support for NATO, and then remove himself from politics by taking his name out of contention for the 1952 campaign. It seemed like a fair trade: If Taft agreed to support NATO and collective security, Eisenhower would support him and the nomination would almost certainly be his.

Before the meeting, Eisenhower took the time to write out a statement that would, unequivocally, remove himself from the nominating process. "Having been called back to military duty," he wrote, "I want to announce that my name may not be used by anyone as a candidate for President—and if they do I will repudiate such efforts."[1] Gone were the little equivocations, the carefully chosen words that left the nation wondering whether he really wanted to be president or not. But the meeting with Taft did little more than produce further animosity between the Eisenhower and Taft. Taft made it clear that he would not support NATO, and that he did not believe that Truman had the authority to send troops to Europe in peacetime without the consent of Congress. Eisenhower argued that the president did, indeed, have that power, and that he was immediately requesting several divisions. He recalled in his memoir that he "insisted on an answer regarding support of the collective principle. I failed to get an assurance. . . . My disappointment was acute," he continued. "I was resentful toward those who seemed to me to be playing politics in matters I thought vital to America and the Free World." Taft left the meeting—taking with him the only chance he would ever have to become President of the United States.[2] Eisenhower had spent the war trying to convince various disparate forces to work together against the common enemy of Nazi Germany. He had also thrown his full support toward the formation of the United Nations, the world's primary instrument of collective security and internationalism. Taft, the prewar isolationist-turned postwar unilateralist, opposed all that. To Eisenhower, Taft worked for tighter budgets, even at the expense of military spending.

Following the meeting, Eisenhower commented to an aide that it "might be more effective to keep some aura of mystery around my future personal plans. For the moment," he added, "I decided to remain silent, not to declare myself out as a potential political factor. . . . The statement I had drafted was so unequivocal that if I had carried out my intentions of publicizing it, my political life would have ended without ever starting. The paper was destroyed."[3]

Eisenhower may have had some secret desire to be president, but he still did not like the idea of running a campaign, of seeking political office, and of climbing into the political arena and undertaking the nasty fight of dirty politics. In November 1949, while at Columbia and just a year after the 1948 election, he was still complaining. "I do not want any political office," he confided to his diary, "even if it could be handed to me without effort on my part." He added that he sensed "no obligation, of any kind, to run for office. . . . Every day," he continued "this question comes before me in some way or another. Personal letters, visitors, request for addresses, etc., etc. I'm worn out trying to explain myself." He included a list of names of those who had been coming to see him regularly. They included Tom Dewey; influential journalist and politician, Clare Boothe Luce; Eisenhower's wartime chief of staff and confidant, Walter Bedell Smith (representing a group that he described as "big industrialists"); oil man Pete Jones; investment banker Bill Burnham; and New York *Herald-Tribune* vice president, Bill Robinson.[4]

Dewey's unexpected defeat in 1948 almost certainly spurred Eisenhower to look at the possibility of running in the 1952 campaign. He had decided to stay out of the 1948 election for a number of reasons. If nothing else, he lacked an effective political organization and the money to win the nomination and the campaign. At the same time, he and Dewey thought much alike. Both were moderate Republicans, internationalists, with similar views toward organized labor, race, and most other domestic issues.[5]

But as the 1952 campaign approached, Dewey was a two-time loser. Certainly, he could have made a third run, but generally American party leaders are not willing to tap a candidate three times. This meant that the Republicans would almost certainly turn to Taft, the Ohio conservative, the leader of the Republican Old Guard.

At the other end, it looked like Truman might try and make another run. And even though Eisenhower was Truman's direct subordinate and the direct purveyor of White House policy on the international front, he had little respect for the president. To Eisenhower, Truman was the worst sort of politician; he wallowed in the mud of politics, worked only to achieve the goal of being elected, and, Eisenhower believed, he damaged the good offices of the presidency. "[P]oor Truman," Eisenhower wrote in his diary. "A fine man who, in the middle of a stormy lake, knows nothing of swimming. Yet a lot of drowning people are forced to look to him as a life guard. If his wisdom could only equal his good intent!"[6] To Eisenhower, the choices for Americans in 1952 might well be between Taft and Truman. There were really no other big players on the horizon for either party. Eisenhower must certainly have considered the consequences for the nation if he simply chose to sit on the sidelines again and watch political events unfold.

In late October 1951, Eisenhower received a letter from two important figures in the Republican Party: Ernest T. Weir, who headed the National Steel Corporation, and Harold Talbot, a party insider. They told Eisenhower that if he did not make a run, then Taft would take the nomination, perhaps even before the convention began. And then in the general election, he would "get no votes from anybody under 30 years of age." They added that he would lose the election to Truman, and "four years more of Democratic . . . government

. . . will put us so far on the road to socialism that there will be no return to free enterprise."[7]

At the same time, there was the decades-old adage that "Taft can't win," the belief that Robert Taft was an effective leader in the Senate, a strong representative for the conservative state of Ohio, but that he did not have the personal appeal needed to win a national election. It was as much an assumption as it was a campaign slogan used against Taft since he made it clear that he had presidential ambitions. All of this must have pushed Eisenhower further toward making the run.

As the head of NATO, it was Eisenhower's duty to stay out of politics. Army regulation number 600-10 made this clear. In his current position, he could not participate in a political campaign. There is no evidence in the record that Truman appointed Eisenhower to the NATO command simply to keep him out of the 1952 political arena. Eisenhower was, after all, the best man for the job of NATO commander, perhaps the only man qualified to lead the West as the clouds of the Cold War began to form. However, if Truman intended to run in 1952, Eisenhower, as a Republican, would certainly present a formidable foe, one best kept in Paris and in control of the West's primary military force, and out of the political fray.

Through most of 1950 and well into 1951, Eisenhower continued to deny that he was a candidate for president. But by 1951 his tone changed. He stopped insisting that he would not run, and that he would not be a candidate; he began talking about a call to duty, and that he would not seek a nomination but, perhaps, accept one under certain circumstances. For instance, in a note to Charlie White, the president of Republic Steel, Eisenhower wrote, "I always insisted that I would never be connected in any way with politics . . . except in such exceptional circumstances where a duty was clearly indicated."[8] In the meantime, several groups had formed, mostly behind the scenes, to further Eisenhower's candidacy. Perhaps the most important of these was headed by Senator James Duff of Pennsylvania. Duff called himself a liberal Republican and saw himself more in the mold of the early-century progressive Republicans than a modern member of the Republican Party. To Duff, Taft was anathema, the very personification of what was wrong with the Republican Party at mid-century. Working with Duff was a group of "liberal" Republicans who considered Eisenhower to be, like themselves, a liberal Republican and the future of the party. Leading this group was General Edwin N. Clark, West Point graduate, New York lawyer, and wartime supply chief; and Russell Davenport, the chief editor at Henry Luce's *Fortune*.

This group also included such names as Vermont Senator Ralph Flanders, Maine Senator Margaret Chase Smith, Massachusetts Senator Henry Cabot Lodge, magazine editor Henry Luce and his wife, Tom Dewey, New Jersey Representative Clifford Case, Duff, Kentucky Senator John Sherman Cooper,

Coca-Cola head Robert Woodruff of Georgia, Representative (and past chairman of the Republican National Committee) Hugh Scott of Pennsylvania, Arizona Governor Howard Pyle, New Mexico cattle rancher Albert Mitchell, Wyoming Governor Frank Barrett, journalist Palmer Hoyt, Nebraska Governor Val Peterson, among others. Many of these liberal Republicans had cut their political teeth on the ill-fated Wendell Willkie campaign in 1940. Willkie had died in 1944 and his (supposed) liberal philosophy of infusing new blood into the old New Deal programs had generally lost its credibility as the Republican Right began to build muscle inside the party in the immediate postwar years. By about 1951, many of these liberal Republicans had become the disaffected, the outcasts in a newly revived party of conservatives from the Midwest and their even more conservative allies in the West. To people like Clark, Davenport, Duff, and other Northeasterners, Eisenhower was their key to the future, a new liberal candidate, a Republican who would take the party out of the hands of the Taftites and return it to its rightful owners.

By late summer and early fall of 1951, this group had convinced Eisenhower that running a campaign on his behalf without his own endorsement, indeed, while he continued to insist publicly that he was not a candidate, was difficult. Local politicos refused to give their support, statewide delegates to the Republican convention refused to leave Taft's side for Eisenhower, and fund raising for a candidate who may or may not run proved almost impossible. In late September, Eisenhower let those supporters know that they were on their own: "I am engaged in a terribly important job," he told Pennsylvania Representative and supporter Hugh Scott. "I [have taken this] job at considerable personal risk. If there are people at home who feel that a cause is worth pursuing, then they ought to be willing to accept whatever risk is incident to making that fight for that cause."[9] About a month later, in mid-October, at Clark's insistence, Eisenhower agreed to write a short, secret, memorandum to James Duff that stated unequivocally that he was a Republican, that he would "do nothing to gain a nomination," but, he added, "I will enter no objection of any kind to your pursuing whatever course . . . you may deem proper in organizing like-minded people." The letter was intended for Duff's personal use, to allow him to tell prospective supporters that Eisenhower would make the run. This letter, Eisenhower continued, is not "for general use . . . because . . . it is of the highest importance to our country that the American Commander in this post as Supreme Allied Commander remain absolutely aloof from partisan politics." He then concluded with a point that made it clear that he had been on a candidate's path for some time: "I realize that I have told you, herein, nothing that you have not always known over the past three years or so."[10]

One minor problem had already begun to emerge in the fledgling Eisenhower campaign: Duff and Dewey could not get along. The two men held many of the same basic convictions, but at the 1948 Republican convention, Duff mounted an anti-Dewey campaign that popularized a slogan, "anybody but Dewey."[11] If Dewey decided not to make a run in 1952, which it seemed he would not, he was certainly powerful enough to push Duff to the sidelines. So it was decided that the two Republican moderates would work together to choose a leader of the Eisenhower campaign. After rejecting a few choices, all agreed that the campaign should be run by Henry Cabot Lodge, Jr. Lodge, a Massachusetts Senator and moderate, had always admired Eisenhower, and as early as 1950 he had encouraged him to make a run for president. He was, by most accounts, something of a compromise candidate, someone who could get along with all sides of the burgeoning Eisenhower candidacy. And, of course, Eisenhower liked him.[12]

Much of this was still quiet. In fact, Eisenhower continued to insist, publicly, that he would refuse to "seek" a candidacy. But in early January 1952, he announced that he was, in fact, a Republican, and that he would accept a draft from the Republican Party if it was offered. This was in direct response to several inquiries by Republican operatives who wanted to place Eisenhower's name on the ballot in New Hampshire.[13] However, he added, "under no circumstances will I ask for relief from [NATO command] in order to seek nomination for political office and I shall not participate in pre-convention activities of others who may have such an intention with respect to me." In addition, he added, "in the absence . . . of a clear-cut call to political duty I shall continue to devote my full attention and energies to the performance of the vital task to which I am assigned."[14] Statements of this sort may seem insincere: he was clearly allowing his candidacy to go forward from behind the scenes while denying any desire to run for the office. But Eisenhower truly seemed to believe what he said. He had an important job as the supreme commander of the newly formed NATO; the Cold War was just taking shape, and there seemed to be a genuine military threat from the Communist east. "For me to admit, while in this post, or to imply or even to leave open for interpretation by others a partisan political loyalty would properly be resented by thinking Americans and would be doing a disservice to our country, for it would interfere with the job to which the country has assigned me."[15]

Eisenhower's next step was the New Hampshire primary. His supporters insisted he run. He agreed, but only if his name could be placed in contention by others. He would not, of course, campaign. New Hampshire Governor Sherman Adams begged Lodge for assistance. Adams had agreed to orchestrate the Eisenhower effort in New Hampshire, but as late as December 1951, he still was not even certain if Eisenhower was a Republican.[16] In his response, Lodge insisted that Eisenhower was, in fact, a Republican. He also quoted Army Regulation 600-10 that did "not allow Eisenhower to participate in a campaign in his position." However, Lodge concluded, "he would consider a call to political service by the will of the party and the people to be the highest form of duty."[17] Eisenhower recognized the difficulty of Lodge's position. "I keenly realize that I am of no direct help in all the matters of policy and decision with which you are continually faced. But, I feel, on the other hand, that as long as I am performing a national duty. . . . I am possibly providing as much ammunition for your guns as I could in any other way."[18]

Finally, Eisenhower agreed to allow his name to be placed on the ballot in New Hampshire. In his political memoir, *Mandate for Change*, he called this a turning point. "[F]or the first time I had allowed the smallest break in a regular practice of returning a flat refusal to any kind of proposal that I become an active participant."[19] On January 5, Lodge announced that he would arrange to have Eisenhower's name placed on the New Hampshire ballot. But Eisenhower still held back. "I'm willing to go part way in trying to recognized a 'duty,'" he wrote in his diary just a few days later, "but I do not have to seek one—and I will not."[20]

Eisenhower wanted to run, and he probably wanted to be president, but he seemed to be looking for something that would make it clear that there was a grassroots campaign, or some sort of groundswell that truly commanded that he give up his job in Europe and answer the greater call to duty in politics. That evidence seemed to come when Jacqueline Cochran brought with her to Eisenhower's home in Paris a film of an Eisenhower-for-president rally that she and her husband had organized at Madison Square Garden in New York. Cochran was an interesting figure. Perhaps bested only by Amelia Earhart as the nation's foremost aviatrix, Cochran had organized women pilots during the war to deliver planes from their manufacturing points in the United States to the war in Europe. In February 1952, she and her husband, RKO Pictures CEO Floyd Odlum, flew the film across the Atlantic for the purpose of showing Eisenhower that the public did, if fact, want him to run.[21]

The film of the Madison Square Garden rally was a full two hours long hours. The film's purpose was to show Eisenhower that Taft was in the lead in acquiring convention delegates, and Minnesota Governor Harold Stassen (who most believed was a stand-in for Eisenhower) had deserted the Eisenhower camp and was now running a fairly successful campaign on his own. In the Madison Square Garden film, Ethel Merman sang "There's No Business Like Show Business," and Mary Martin sang "I'm in Love with a Wonderful Guy." A wash tub was handed around with the slogan emblazed on the side, "Holler with Your Dollar." By some accounts, over 19,000 attended the Eisenhower-for-president rally, and as many as 7,000 additional supporters were turned away.[22]

Again, Eisenhower wanted to run. He had made that pretty clear through several statements, but his dealings had been with politicians and business leaders. All had told him that he could win; all he had to do was step forward, take the reins of the campaign, win the Republican nomination, and then the general election. But his statements to the press (and in private) had always been concluded with statements such as "in the absence of a clear-cut call to political duty," he would remain at this post in Europe. He seemed to want to run, and he confirmed that his support was deeper than the politicians and businessmen who passed through his office, people who (so he thought) often had something to gain personally from his candidacy. The Cochran film seemed to give him what he needed, and it pushed him over the top. "The [film] brought by Miss Cochran was very elaborate and long," he wrote in his diary the next day.

> Viewing it finally developed into a real emotional experience for Mamie and me. I've not been so upset in years. Clearly to be seen is the mass longing of America of some kind of reasonable solution for her nagging, persistent and almost terrifying problems. It is a real experience to realize that one could become a symbol for many thousands of the hope they have!![23]

About a month later he wrote to Cochran, thanking her for her efforts on his behalf: "The knowledge that so many Americans are devoting their time and energy in an effort to obtain for me a position of high civilian leadership brings me a feeling of pride and a deep sense of humility."[24]

While there were those who pushed Eisenhower to run (and thus to leave the NATO command for the greater good of the nation), there were others who advised him to stay put, and that the nomination and the presidency would eventually come to him. The objective was the same; the method of achievement was just different. William Robinson, one of Eisenhower's close personal friends and golf buddies, told Eisenhower often that it was not necessary to return home to campaign. In mid-March, Robinson wrote to Eisenhower that he could win the Republican nomination, even if he waited until after the convention to return to the United States. He added that doing what needed to be done in Europe was an important task, one that voters will understand.[25] "As of right now," Robinson wrote about a week later, "there is no higher duty *here* than there is *there*."[26] Herbert Brownell, another Eisenhower insider, recalled later that Eisenhower may have been seeing all this from a different angle. "I think he had it in his mind . . . that it would be a possibility that if he ran that he would stay in Europe and there would be a draft by the convention and that then he could make up his mind at that point whether or not he would accept."[27] In other words, he may have wanted to be *both* the NATO commander *and* a candidate for the presidency.

On January 6, Lodge, during a press conference in Washington, was asked (as he had been asked many times before) if Eisenhower would run. His response was cryptic: "Ask him and see." The reporters called Paris. Eisenhower issued a statement on January 8. The letter, published in *The New York Times*, was not an announcement of his candidacy, but it was all his supporters needed. He would finally make the run. "Senator Lodge's announcement of yesterday

. . . gives an accurate account of the general tenor of my political convictions and of my Republican voting record." However, he added, "under no circumstances will I ask for relief from this assignment in order to seek nomination to political office and I shall not participate in the pre-convention activities of others who may have such an intention with respect to me."[28]

The 1952 New Hampshire primary was that nation's first, and it had special meaning in postwar American politics. The primary had been a part of the American electoral scene since Woodrow Wilson ran there unopposed in 1916, but in 1949 the state simplified its ballot access laws in an effort to increase voter turnout. At the same time, the press had begun to see the New Hampshire primary as something of a bellwether, a portent for the national campaign to come. Taft was entered and, by most accounts, he was poised to win the primary on his way to the party nomination. On the Democratic side, Tennessee Senator Estes Kefauver had entered in a direct challenge to President Truman. The primary was set for the second Tuesday in March, that is, March 11. If Eisenhower chose to sit out the New Hampshire primary, the winners would probably be Taft and Truman. The prospect for Eisenhower of those two candidates winning their respective party nominations and then running against each other in the general election in November was, again, probably more than he could take.[29]

Eisenhower was not one to throw his weight into a campaign. However, a discernible lack of action had hurt him (and the Republican Party) in the past—and it would hurt the party in the future. Two election cycles later, in 1960, Eisenhower could have thrown his considerable influence behind his vice president, Richard Nixon, in his campaign against John Kennedy. He did not, and Kennedy won. In 1964, Eisenhower was the Republican Party's elder statesman, and he could easily have influenced the Republican Party nomination that year. Again, he did not, and Barry Goldwater was nominated, a candidate he opposed as too conservative and unelectable. Eisenhower then stayed out of that campaign, and Goldwater was crushed by Lyndon Johnson's reelection. Often Eisenhower managed events, famously from behind the scenes. But other times, he simply stood away and allowed events to take their natural course without his input.

As the New Hampshire primary approached, there were still those in his party who were uncertain of Eisenhower's intentions. *The New York Times* reported that it was in this period that as many as 100 people visited Eisenhower's headquarters in France each week. Most tried to convince him to come home and campaign.[30] It was in these days (the spring of 1952) that Eisenhower may have been convinced to run by John Foster Dulles. Dulles would be Eisenhower's secretary of state and the president's primary confidant on foreign policy issues. Dulles had also served as an informal foreign policy advisor to the Republican Party during the Roosevelt years.

According to Sherman Adams, Dulles told Eisenhower that together "they would make the greatest team in history." In Adams's words, that was a "pretty persuasive argument." It was Lodge, however, who finally told Adams that he had the authority to place Eisenhower's name on the ballot. The candidate would not, of course, be there to campaign.[31] Eisenhower had until February 10 to have his name removed from the ballot. "To most politicians," *The New York Times* remarked, his silence signified his availability.[32]

Even then, with his hat clearly in the ring, Eisenhower refused to acknowledge that he would seek the nomination. In his diary on January 10, he wrote, "Time and again I've told anyone who'd listen that I will not seek a nomination. I don't give a d— how impossible a 'draft' may be. I'm willing to go part way in trying to recognize a 'duty,' but I do not have to seek one, and I will not." Earlier in the same entry, however, he wrote, "I would so consider a nomination by the Republican party."[33]

Eisenhower's willingness to run but refusal to return from Europe and campaign worried a few of his supporters. In a memorandum following a meeting of the top Republican Party minds, William Robinson wrote about his frustrations, "I'm personally . . . concerned about the outcome [of the nomination] unless heroic measures are taken to sustain and enhance public opinion in favor of the general." He added that "it is now crystal-clear that two-thirds of the professional politicians [in the Republican Party] who will control delegates not only want Taft but are becoming a little more convinced every day that he can not only become nominated but be elected." The argument that Taft can't win, he continued, "is losing its potency."[34]

By all accounts, Taft was a shoe-in in New Hampshire. He had even decided not to campaign there. MacArthur had originally decided to make a run for the nomination in New Hampshire, but he just as quickly withdrew and then made a statement that *Time* magazine concluded was an endorsement for Taft: "The immediate demand upon the citizens lies in the selection of a national leadership of demonstrated ability in the science of civil government."[35] But Taft believed he would win in New Hampshire, even if he did not win a majority of the votes. If he could secure a place closely behind Eisenhower, he could claim a moral victory over a popular military hero who had little business in the political arena. If he won a majority of the votes he could, of course, claim an outright victory over Eisenhower. In the final count, however, Taft was mauled. The absent Eisenhower took a commanding 50.4 percent (and all the New Hampshire delegates) to Taft's anemic 38.7 percent.

A week later, in Minnesota, Eisenhower-as-vote-getter pulled a huge upset when (in a nonbinding write-in campaign) over 108,000 voters wrote his name on their ballots. Harold Stassen won the primary with 129,000 votes. Taft, like Eisenhower, was also not on the ballot. He received only

24,093 write-in votes.[36] American voters who had not been concerned before began paying attention.

Eisenhower had told Lodge and others that he had hoped he would not have to return to the United States until after the Republican convention. Clearly, he wanted to be handed the nomination by acclamation and avoid the dirty struggles of politics.[37] Eisenhower often told the press that he would not give up his job at NATO in the "absence of a compelling call . . . by a higher authority." A reporter for *Time* asked for the definition of a "compelling call." It would be, Eisenhower said, one "that is traditionally and universally recognized as the voice of the American people speaking through a national convention. "Such a call," he added, "imposes an obligation of citizenship on the man so honored." *Time* translated: "In other words, Ike will come home and campaign if he gets the GOP nomination."[38]

In late February, when MacArthur dropped out and then announced that he would throw his support to Taft, Eisenhower's demeanor seemed to change. In his diary, just following MacArthur's announcement, he wrote, "[I]f they will leave me alone it is possible that I can soon (several months) turn this job over to another."[39] About a year later, following his victory in the general election, he recalled in his diary of these events and how he felt at the time: "[A]fter being [at NATO] less than a year, the pressures from political figures became so great that again I was persuaded that I had a duty to turn to another task, that of offering myself as a political leader to unseat the New Deal-Fair Deal bureaucracy in Washington."[40]

Those around Eisenhower in the spring of 1952 had tried to convince him that Taft would take the nomination by default if he did not return at once and take the reins of his campaign. On April 2, he wrote to Secretary of Defense Robert Lovett: "I request that you initiate my appropriate release from assignment . . . by approximately June 1, and that I be placed on inactive status upon my return to the United States."[41] In mid-April, he announced to the press that he would resign from the military and return to run for president.[42] Later that month, he wrote a personal letter to Truman asking to be allowed to retire from the military. He added that he was surprised by the developments that had injected him into the world of politics, and that the political events had begun to interfere with his military duties.[43] On May 21, he delivered what is usually called his "Farewell to NATO" speech. He returned, first to Washington, where Truman gave him a quick tour of the newly renovated White House and then in a short ceremony, the president pinned a fourth oak leaf cluster on his Distinguished Service Medal. From there he went to the Pentagon for lunch with Secretary Lovett. It was there, by most accounts, that Eisenhower changed from his uniform into civilian cloths and began his campaign for the presidency.[44]

Then, on June 4 he returned to his hometown of Abilene, Kansas, and delivered his first speech as a candidate. This event may have been the first nationally televised speech of its kind. The event is most remembered for the rainstorm that interrupted his words and sent the crowd scattering for cover. But in this speech, and another several days later in Denver, Eisenhower laid down his vision for the nation—really for the first time. He identified the nation's problems as high taxes and the growth of federal power. Then he spoke of "evils," those things that he saw as a danger to the nation's future and to its very character: disunity, inflation, excessive taxation, and increased bureaucracy. He continued by pointing to the specter of world communism, and his frustration that the Yalta agreements had been negotiated and signed in secret. Then he added a point that may seem insignificant, but it was important to a lot of Americans at the time: "[O]ne party has been in power too long in this country." In Denver, a few days later (in 97-degree heat) he told a crowd of some 10,000 that the nation could no longer afford to be isolationist, and that it was the United Nations that held the key to the future of American foreign policy.[45] These speeches did not ring the bells of American politics. They were fairly mundane and often described as middle of the road and boring. But they made up what would become the foundations of Eisenhower's philosophy of American government. Through the entire next decade, his two terms in office, he would seldom vary from these basic principles of politics, economics, and foreign policy.

It was pretty clear through the first two years of the decade that Eisenhower wanted to be president, and that he would accept a draft by the Republican Party if it was offered. But because of his obligation at NATO, and Army Regulation 600-10, he believed that he should avoid all statements that might place him into the realm of politics. At the same time, the Cold War was just beginning, and to most Americans that was the defining factor of the age. If the United States was about to go to war with the Soviet Union, who better to head Allied forces than Eisenhower himself? Why would he leave that post and throw himself into the political arena? At the same time, Eisenhower probably came to believe that the nation was faced with a future that included a choice between Truman and Taft, two people whose policies he could not abide. He tried to stand aside and allow the Republican nomination to come to him, but when that was, clearly, not going to happen, he announced his retirement from the military, flew home, and began campaigning for the presidency. He could do nothing else.

Chapter 4

Truman Decides Not to Run

Truman could run again in 1952. Prior to 1951 the two-term presidency had only been a tradition (broken only by Franklin Roosevelt's four victories). The Twenty-second Amendment to the Constitution limited presidents to two elections—thus two full terms in office. But it was also included that "this article shall not apply to any person holding the office of President when this article was proposed by Congress." Truman was, of course, in office when the amendment was proposed in 1947—the amendment was finally ratified in February 1952. Truman had succeeded Roosevelt in April 1945 and then won only one election in November 1948. Would he run again in 1952? Could he pull off another upset like the one he orchestrated in 1948? Most of those closest to him thought he could not.

As early as November 1951, Truman seemed to have made the decision not to run in 1952. He would later backpedal on that decision when it appeared that there was no prominent Democrat waiting in the wings to succeed him. But in late 1951, while in Key West, he read a memorandum to his staff, stating unequivocally that he would not run in 1952. Robert Dennison, one of Truman's top aides, recalled the event in a letter to Walt Rostow some twenty years later. "I was present . . . at Key West in November 1951 when [Truman] read his memorandum to us," Dennison recalled. "I was seated beside the President and when he finished reading I asked to see the memorandum so I could be sure my ears had not deceived me. . . . [N]one of us disclosed his decision and it was not until . . . March 1952 that the country was aware of it."[1]

In another instance, within a few weeks, Truman had again stated that he would not run, and again everyone involved kept the secret. Through the later months of 1951, journalist William Hillman was in the process of interviewing the president for his book, *Mr. President.* Following the some twenty-four interview sessions at Blair House, Truman's own stenographer, Jack Romagna, told one of Truman's press secretaries, "that on January 9, the President disclosed flatly to Hillman that he would not be a candidate for re-election."[2]

It was probably a good decision for Truman. He was not in a good place as the 1952 campaign began. The war in Korea was not going well; the U.S. military was not losing there, but it was also not winning. The Chinese had unexpectedly entered the war in late 1950; there were repeated setbacks on the battlefield, and most of the problems were being blamed (most likely incorrectly) on what was perceived as the newly coddled generation of soldiers who just could not cut the mustard in a war of attrition on the Asian mainland. In addition, just after the 1948 campaign, Truman was forced to dismiss his secretary of defense, James Forrestal. Forrestal had met, clandestinely, with Governor Dewey just before the 1948 campaign, probably under the assumption that Dewey would win the election and keep Forrestal on as secretary of defense. When that became apparent to Truman, mostly through an expose' in the press, Truman asked Forrestal to resign. His successor, Louis Johnson, immediately shouldered much of the criticism for the U.S. military's lack of success in Korea. In mid-September, Truman replaced Johnson with General George C. Marshall. By April of the next year, Truman was forced to make an unpopular decision when he dismissed General Douglas MacArthur as commander of all forces in Korea following a conflict with MacArthur over the conduct of the war. All of these events damaged Truman's presidency. He had gotten the nation into a war that he could not win, at first with the North Koreans and then with the Chinese, all the while insisting that it was not, in fact, a war at all, but a "police action." As the 1952 campaign ramped up, Truman's war in Korea had become a political liability.

Truman was also having a great deal of difficulty with the expanding economy. He had decided not to strengthen price controls at the beginning of the Korean War, and that led to immediate inflation. Then in January 1951, he froze prices. That did not work. By 1952, prices had jumped to record levels. Some wanted strict controls to keep consumer prices in check, while others wanted prices to rise in order to increase profits. Truman tried to hold the line, walk the fence. The result, not surprisingly, was that he made everyone mad.

On the domestic front, the situation was not much better. Harry Vaughn, Truman insider and White House military aide, was accused in the press of funneling funds to a racetrack developer in 1946. Arkansas Senator J. William Fulbright began an investigation of that event and eventually uncovered some misconduct inside the Reconstruction Finance Corporation. There was little there to be concerned about, but photos in the press of the wives of the accused wrongdoers wearing mink coats hurt Truman. All of this seemed very close to the president, but Truman really had no knowledge of any of the events.

However, he could have cut his losses early, and fired everyone involved, but he refused. His lack of action on the issue damaged his presidency and, then, finally it may have inhibited his decision to run in 1952.

Truman had also gotten into trouble over the appointment of William Boyle to head the Democratic National Committee. Boyle was a product of the old Pendergast machine, the notoriously corrupt Kansas City political machine that had raised Truman from local to national politician. In 1951, Boyle also got mixed up in a loan scandal, and to make matters worse for the Truman administration, he refused to resign. As Alonzo Hamby has written, "By appointing Boyle, Truman had thrown up a clay pigeon for Republicans, southern Democrats, and anti-administration journalists to blast away at."[3]

Through 1951, Truman was also plagued with revelations of corruption inside the Tax Division of the Internal Revenue Service. As that scandal widened, IRS officials in Washington, and then all over the country, either resigned or were dismissed to avoid indictment and arrest. By the end of 1951, nearly sixty IRS officials had either resigned before an investigation could begin, or had been fired. Again, the incidents were not particularly close to Truman, but he did nothing. His complacency damaged his presidency even further. In early April 1952, Truman fired his attorney general, J. Howard McGrath. Even then, the scandal would not go away. McGrath's successor at Justice, James McGranery, ran headlong into the wave of anticommunism that was sweeping Washington. That kept him away from the Justice Department for weeks following his appointment. The "cleanup" went on, but not before Truman was damaged badly by the events. Critical references to the Truman administration became "that mess in Washington." During the period, Truman's numbers dipped, at one point to a paltry approval rating of just 23 percent.[4]

Despite all these problems (the corruption in Washington, the stalemate in Korea, McCarthy's antics, and even the economic and labor problems he had faced with demobilization) Truman was essentially a politician whose basic instincts were to attack his enemies head on and vindicate himself and his policies by winning the next election—really much as he had done in 1948. But the prospects for such an electoral victory in November were not good. Even his closest advisors—particularly Clark Clifford, who had orchestrated much of the 1948 strategy—were not on board for a 1952 run. "I thought it likely that the tide which he had so brilliantly turned back in 1948 would sweep over him," Clifford recalled in his memoirs. "More important," he added, "I felt his Administration had run out of steam."[5] So Truman began fishing for a successor.

There is even some evidence that Truman may have decided not to run in the 1952 campaign as early as 1950. In the congressional elections that year, Republicans again made big gains. This time it was twenty-eight seats in the House and five seats in the Senate that were lost to the Republicans. It seemed to show that Truman's popularity that had resulted in his 1948 electoral victory was little more than a flash in the pan, a defining moment when all the political planets were aligned and the nation voted for Truman. Before that election, his approval ratings were dismal. By November 1950, the voters were again turning away from the Democrats and looking to a Washington dominated by conservative Republicans. But Truman also may have felt that if he announced his intentions not to run, then he would be destroyed in the press, damaging any chance he might have of picking a successor. His objective was to keep the press in suspense, at least until the year of the election.[6]

It is perhaps the greatest honor for a president to leave office after two terms (in Truman's case, *nearly* two terms) and be able to appoint a successor. It rarely happens in the United States. Usually after eight years, voters want to move in another direction and elect a member of the other party. Truman believed he had done a good job as president. He had ended World War II, tackled Reconversion (and averted another economic depression—as he saw it), and established the United States as the leader of the free world against world communism. He may not have had great success in domestic affairs, but he believed he had carried on the New Deal mantle and strengthened the Democratic Party. Of course, he wanted someone to take over his reigns, to carry on his administration. He wanted a successor who would vindicate his time in office and continue his policies. The problem for Truman in 1952 was that there was no clear choice on the horizon. Potential candidates either were not fit for the job or did not want it. And despite Truman's own views of his time in office, few politicians wanted to carry the heavy burden of the damaged Truman administration into the 1952 campaign.

Truman's first choice (and perhaps his best choice) was Fred Vinson, then Chief Justice of the Supreme Court. Truman and Vinson were best of friends. *The New York Times* recalled their friendship, on the day after Vinson's death in the fall of 1953. "The Vinson family would go to the White House for Thanksgiving dinner with the Trumans." In addition, the *Times* added, "both the President and the Chief Justice had telephones by their beds and regularly held long talks late at night, in which the President received Mr. Vinson's advice and counsel on many problems."[7]

Truman and Vinson were of the same cloth. Truman particularly admired Vinson's abilities to succeed in all three branches of government. Vinson had won election to the House of Representatives six times, had served as Truman's Secretary of the Treasury; and then he was appointed by Truman to replace Harlan Fiske Stone in the Supreme Court. He continued to support Truman through the worst of times, and when the Supreme Court voided the president's takeover of the steel industry during a contentious labor strike in the spring of 1952, it was Vinson who stood by Truman and wrote the dissenting opinion.[8]

The Truman-Vinson relationship was all the more important in the post-FDR world. Truman's style was not always compatible with those around him. He had tried to include in his administration some of Roosevelt's brightest lights, those figures most associated with the New Deal, people like Henry Wallace, Henry Morganthau, Harold Ickes, and Francis Biddle. But Truman's downhome style and lack of intellectual sophistication simply put him at odds with the New Deal types. Not surprisingly, the old New Dealers fell away, most resigning in quiet protest. In the case of Henry Wallace, however, the split with Truman was so disagreeable and hostile that it caused the Democratic Party to split in the 1948 campaign.

Vinson was something of an anomaly. He was a Southern New Dealer who got along well with Truman. As early as 1950, Truman had told Vinson that if he chose not to run in 1952, Truman hoped Vinson would agree to be his successor. In mid-October 1951, Truman agreed to offer Vinson his full support if he would make the run. Vinson took three days to make a decision and then turned Truman down flat. He cited his lack of political skills—now out of politics since he left the House of Representatives in the late 1930s—and his health. At age sixty-three, Vinson only had a year to live.[9]

With that, Truman began looking around for someone else, a number-two choice. There is even some evidence that he approached Eisenhower again (as he had in 1948) and offered to support him in 1952 if he would run as a Democrat.[10] When that turned out to be a political dead end, Truman began looking elsewhere. In a series of notes, he wrote during the next summer (July 1952) Truman recalled his thinking. Georgia Senator Richard Russell was interested in running, but Truman realized that "he is poison to Northern Democrats and honest liberals. I doubt if he could carry a single state north of the Ohio River. . . . There is no chance for Dick." Then Truman turned to his vice president and old friend, Ablen Barkley, who was about to turn seventy-five. "He can't see," Truman wrote. "He shows his age. I wish he could be 64 instead of 75. . . . It takes him 5 minutes to sign his name and as President he'd have to sign his name 600 times a day. . . . My good friend Alben would be dead in three months if he should inherit my job." He even considered Averill Harriman, his own secretary of commerce, the son of railroad mogul E. H. Harriman, and a prominent financier. Even though Harriman had never held an elected office, Truman still liked the man. "He is the ablest of them all." But Truman added, "Can we elect a Wall Street banker and a railroad tycoon President of the United States on the Democratic ticket?" Truman thought not.[11]

On January 10, with no real successor in sight, Truman again considered a run. In a press conference he said that he would make the run himself if Taft won the Republican nomination.[12] Then, later in the month, with the New Hampshire primary just weeks away, he was asked if he would enter any primaries—obviously in anticipation of running for the Democratic nomination. He replied that he did not need to run in primaries. They were, he said, nothing more than "eyewash," and, he added, "when it comes to the national convention meeting, [primaries do] not mean a thing." Despite his comments, Truman did nothing to remove his name from the New Hampshire primary ballot.[13]

At about that same time, in late January 1952, Truman invited Illinois Governor Adlai Stevenson to Blair House for lunch. Truman and Stevenson were very different. Truman's downhome, up-from-his-bootstraps ways hardly appealed to Stevenson, and Truman probably saw Stevenson's intellectual demeanor in the same light as the haughty New Dealers whom he had come to despise. But Truman had been impressed with Stevenson's speeches; he appreciated his Midwest background and his political heritage (Stevenson's grandfather had been vice president under Grover Cleveland, a president admired by Truman; and a more distant relative had been Abraham Lincoln's campaign manager). Stevenson was perceived as progressive, he hailed from a major industrial state, and he was a champion of honest government. He was also the young new face in the party. But perhaps most important was Stevenson's 1948 victory in Illinois (that probably carried Truman over the top in that crucial state), and his undying support for Truman in 1952 when most of the nation's Democrats were abandoning the president for just about anyone who would take up the party standard. Stevenson was clearly a winner, and as a second choice, he would do.[14]

George Ball, Stevenson's close friend, arranged the meeting, and it was Ball who had been pushing Stevenson to meet Truman and consider Truman's offer. Ball, in fact, drove Stevenson to Blair House to meet the president. According to Ball, when the two men met, Truman said to Stevenson, "Adlai, if a knucklehead like me can be President and not do too badly, think what a really educated smart guy like you could do in the job."[15] But Stevenson balked at the offer. As Truman recalled it,

> [I] offered to have him nominated by the Democratic convention in July. I had to explain to him that any president can control his party's convention. Then I cited Jackson, Hayes, Teddy Roosevelt, Wilson, Franklin Roosevelt, and myself at Philadelphia in 1948. I reminded him that Washington picked Adams, that Jefferson did the same with Madison and Monroe. . . . I told him I could get him nominated whether he wanted to be or not. Then I asked what he'd do in that case.

According to Truman, Stevenson responded that "no patriot could say no to such a condition." But to Truman's surprise, Stevenson did just that; he said he would not run. Truman responded that he was "flabbergasted."[16] By another account, Stevenson was caught off guard by the offer; he responded by expressing doubt, and then asked for some time to think it over. After the meeting, he told George Ball that he had "made a hash" of the entire discussion with Truman, but at the same time he was satisfied that the president had written him off as hopeless and that the incident was closed.[17]

On March 4, Truman and Stevenson met again at Blair House. The meeting was clandestine; Stevenson had, in fact, left St. Louis by airplane under an assumed name.[18] This time, Stevenson tried to make his position clearer. The "no" was straight and firm. As Truman recalled it, Stevenson came to Washington to "tell me that he had made a commitment to run for re-election in Illinois and that he did not think he could go back on that commitment honorably. . . . But I felt," Truman added, "that in Stevenson I had found the man to whom I could safely turn over the responsibilities of party leadership. Here was the kind of man the Democratic party needed."[19] Truman never understood that Stevenson really had no interest in running for president, at least not in March, 1952. Carl McGowan, a Chicago attorney close to Stevenson, recalled in later years: "He told Truman no. And . . . Truman immediately tightened up." The March 4 meeting, he continued, "wasn't much of an interview. Truman was still bemused by [his victory in] 1948 and thought no Republican would ever be elected. He thought the laying on of hands meant electing the President, and saying no was an insult to the office if not to himself."[20]

By that time, Truman was probably convinced that he should not run. A few days later, he headed off on a twenty-day vacation to Key West, Florida, to the "Little White House," as the press called his vacation spot. His name had been placed on the ballot in the New Hampshire primary with the result that he was beaten by Tennessee Senator Estes Kefauver. Kefauver had slogged through the snow and mud of the New Hampshire winter, shaking hands and asking for votes. He won by collecting nearly 20,000 votes and capturing all eight delegates, while embarrassing Truman who pulled in less than 16,000 votes. Truman refused to suffer Kefauver, at best a Senate lightweight with few credentials or discernible abilities. "He served in the House from his own State," Truman recalled, "and had no reputation for anything in particular, but his being unable to understand what was going on when the House was in session. He has the same sort of reputation in the Senate."[21]

Truman's political spirit, perhaps more than anything, almost certainly pushed him to make the run, if only to bury Kefauver and expose his inadequacies. But Clark Clifford, also at Key West, told Truman that it was time to step down, and that the longer he delayed removing his name from contention, the longer it would take for his own allies to mount a strong attack against Kefauver—and the better chance Kefauver had to win the nomination. "I told him frankly," Clifford recalled in his memoirs, "I hoped he would withdraw his name from contention as soon as possible."[22]

Again, Truman seemed to toy with running, or at least he convinced a few of his friends that the possibility was still on the table. In late March, Frank

McKinney, the chairman of the Democratic National Committee, met with Truman and told reporters following the meeting that Truman would run, but only if he could resolve the situation in Korea before the convention. The next day, Truman denied having made the comment to McKinney, and insisted that he would make up his mind and announce his decision when he was good and ready.[23]

Truman had other things to consider. His wife Bess had been by his side as he barnstormed around the nation in 1948. But here, four years later, she balked at another rigorous campaign. She believed Harry had done his job, and that he had nothing to gain by carrying on his administration for another four years. In addition, she believed that she might not survive another four years in Washington, and that Harry might not as well.[24]

Stevenson's problem, as he said over and over, was that he wanted to continue on as governor of Illinois. He had promised to do so, and he intended to keep his promise. At the same time, Stevenson probably did not believe he could beat Eisenhower. And as Eisenhower came closer and closer to running for the Republican nomination, Stevenson pulled away more and more from any call to give up his post as Illinois governor.[25] Perhaps most importantly, however, Stevenson did not want to be associated with Truman. The president's numbers were declining quickly; he was associated with the problems surrounding the war, and the corruption in his administration had fallen directly on him. The last thing the independent-minded Stevenson wanted was to run for president as Truman's candidate, the successor to the tainted Truman administration. Stevenson's reticence in 1952 is often described as indifference and indecisiveness, even an example of the character flaw that dogged him his entire life. But, in fact, Stevenson had several good reasons not to run in 1952, and very few reasons to make the run.

On March 14, Stevenson was called back to Washington. This time he met with Charles Murphy, one of Truman's closest political advisors. Apparently, Murphy was able to place the proper pressure on Stevenson. Following the meeting, Stevenson wrote a letter to Murphy. Not unlike Eisenhower, he would not campaign, he said, but he would accept a draft.[26]

At just about that time, Justice Vinson stepped forward and made a case that Truman should put aside his search for a successor and run himself. To that end, Truman, in late March, invited his closest political advisors to a steak dinner at Blair House.[27] Vinson argued that Truman should run. Clark Clifford, along with as many as twelve others at the meeting, disagreed and pushed Truman to step aside, to allow for new blood in the party.[28] Apparently, Clifford and his cohorts were emphatic in their opinion because Vinson later recalled that it was the frankest meeting he had ever attended. Charles Murphy recalled that the advice not to run was unanimous, but not because they thought Truman would lose. According to Murphy, everyone present assumed that Truman would not only get the Democratic the nomination, but also win the general election if he chose to run. Truman, however, decided that he should not run. He wanted to commemorate the meeting, and he gave each member present a silver dollar minted in 1884.[29]

On March 24, it was announced in *Life* magazine that Truman would probably announce his final decision when he returned from Key West.[30] On March 29, at the annual Jefferson-Jackson Day banquet in Washington, Truman delivered a fighting political speech, attacking the Republicans, suggesting that if they did not reform, they "might die out altogether." Then, to the surprise of many, he announced that he would not run in 1952. "I have served my country long," he said, "and I think efficiently and honestly. I shall not accept a re-nomination. I do not feel that it is my duty to spend another four years in the White House."[31] The audience seemed stunned and confused. There was some applause, mixed with an occasional "no." Truman himself recalled that his announcement was received by "No's and tears. When I arrived at the White House after the announcement I found the ushers and door men almost in tears and the two maids . . . were weeping sure enough."[32] Truman had announced his intentions without a positive answer from Stevenson, but he probably knew that Stevenson would finally, in the end, make the run. The pressure on Stevenson was great, from several angles. Truman surely believed that it was only a matter of time. Leaving the stage, he may have thought, was the best way to give Stevenson the room he needed to run.

Stevenson continued to deny that he would be a candidate, while at the same time he did nothing to stop those working for his candidacy. Just a few weeks before the Democratic National Convention, in late May, Stevenson responded to the "Will you run?" question on "Meet the Press," and said that he only wanted to be governor of Illinois. He said here (and other places) that he would "cross that bridge when I come to it."[33] Perhaps he failed to realize that he was at that bridge, and it was time to either cross it or turn around. As late as July 11, just two weeks before the convention, he was still writing to friends and insisting that he did not want the Democratic nomination.[34] At the same time, he seemed to want to run, and at times he looked and acted like a candidate on the hustings. He allowed his name to remain on the ballots for the Oregon and California primaries, and he even visited those states just days before their elections. He spoke publicly on civil rights, foreign affairs, and other national issues. And in California he even bothered to attack his opponents.[35]

But Stevenson's reticence seemed to awaken others. On April 22, Harriman announced that he would run. Harriman had served as the American ambassador to the Soviet Union, and then as Truman's secretary of commerce. He had always been a Truman favorite, but Truman believed that the Democratic Party would probably not nominate him. If Stevenson truly decided to stand down and not make a run, Harriman would be the only genuine liberal in the field. And that would probably be enough to garner Truman's endorsement. Truman, however, continued to keep his eyes on Stevenson.

For Truman, the decision was probably pretty clear by as early as 1950. He would not run if he could find a suitable successor. The war in Korea, the "corruption" in his administration, his sagging poll numbers, among other factors, probably told him that 1952 would not be another Truman year. When no successor was apparent, and it looked as though Estes Kefauver would take the nomination by default, he clearly toyed with making a run again— and a victory in 1952 would vanquish his enemies and vindicate his policies. By March 1952, his choices had all fallen away, except Adlai Stevenson, and it was apparent that Stevenson would not make the run unless Truman would take his weak poll numbers and stepped aside. With few choices left, he told the world in March 24, 1952 that he would not make the run. He was not doing much more than stepping aside so Stevenson could step into the breach. Truman's plan worked.

Chapter 5

Democrats on the Periphery

Russell and Kefauver and the Democratic Party Primaries

Stevenson would, of course, be handed the Democratic nomination, whether he wanted it or not. But there were other candidates hoping for the nomination. Senator Estes Kefauver of Tennessee jumped into the campaign in late January, a move that surprised no one.[1] Outside of Tennessee, he had very little name recognition, and he needed to enter as many primaries as possible to show that he could win votes, and that he would make a good candidate for the Democrats. He could not wait on Truman to make up his mind whether or not to run. Even in late 1951, he had made it clear that he would announce his candidacy and not wait to see what Truman would do.[2]

Kefauver was born and raised in a small East Tennessee town and seemed to rise above the poverty to receive a law degree from Yale, and then jump directly into the House of Representatives in 1939. In the House, he made a name for himself (not unlike Harry Truman) as a southerner who had stood by the New Deal when most Southern politicians had begun moving away from Roosevelt and his liberal programs. In his 1948 campaign for the Senate, Kefauver took on the Tennessee boss, E. H. "Boss" Crump. Crump had controlled the politics in Memphis, along with the Tennessee Democratic Party, for most of the first half of the twentieth century, and he disliked the upstart Kefauver. During the campaign, Crump and his cronies accused Kefauver of being a Communist, a "fellow traveler," and finally as "stealthy as a raccoon." In response, Kefauver was scheduled to deliver a televised speech, and he showed up wearing a coon skin cap. In his speech he said, "I may be a pet coon, but I'm not Boss Crump's pet coon." Kefauver was the underdog, down by as much as twenty-five points in the polls at times. But he won the election and adopted the coon skin cap as the symbol of his candidacy—and in fact a symbol of his own political independence.[3] Kefauver's victory was the beginning of the end of Crump's hold on Tennessee Democratic Party politics.

Kefauver is often called a populist, mostly because of his intentions to appeal to the common man. His physical demeanor was usually described as tall and gangly. He had an unusually large nose, and he wore horn-rimmed glasses that made his nose stand out even more. He had risen to popularity the year before the 1952 campaign by chairing a nationally televised investigation into organized crime. That effort gave him the aura of a crusader against crime and corruption. But the Democratic Party bosses (including Truman) disliked Kefauver because his investigations into the workings of organized crime had uncovered a close relationship between the mobsters and nation's big-city Democratic Party political machines. Since most states still chose their delegates to the national convention through their state conventions and caucuses, city and state party bosses were at the forefront of those choices. Kefauver and his investigations made that entire process appear corrupt—which it probably was. Thus, the Democratic Party big wigs, again including Truman, branded Kefauver a political maverick who could not be trusted, and they spurned his candidacy.[4]

In 1950, Kefauver jumped into the national spotlight as the chairman of the Senate Special Committee to Investigate Crime in Interstate Commerce, most popularly known as the "Kefauver Committee." The committee held hearings in fourteen cities and interviewed some 600 witnesses, mostly crime bosses, pimps, drug dealers, and other low-level crime figures. In those early days of television, the medium was just getting its legs and trying to find out what the American people would watch. A Senate crime investigation seemed like a good candidate. The events introduced the nation to the Mafia, its leaders, and its inside workings. Perhaps the Kefauver Committee's most famous witness was Frank Costello (Francesco Castiglia), the then head of the Luciano (later Genovese) crime family, one of the five notorious New York Mafia families. As many as 30 million Americans watched the investigation series that featured Costello. Costello agreed to answer questions from the committee (as opposed to invoking the Fifth Amendment to avoid prosecution) if his face was not shown on television. The result was a series of shots of Frank Costello's hands (instead of his face), nervous, sweaty, wringing as the questions from the Kefauver Committee became more and more damning. Finally, Frank walked out of the hearing.[5]

These hearings made Kefauver a national household name, and placed him into the category of a crusader against corruption. He had exposed the Mafia, and he had beaten Crump in Tennessee. He had also cultivated a reputation as a supporter of civil rights for African Americans (from a Southern state), a supporter of organized labor, and a consumer rights advocate. In the very early 1950s, this translated into presidential timber.

But Kefauver was not universally loved, not even in his own party. When he first arrived in Washington, just after the war, he wrote a widely circulated article in *The Journal of Politics* that was little more than a complaint about the time-honored system of seniority in the House of Representatives. Clearly, he did not like being a junior member of the House with few privileges and fewer opportunities. The article offered his own plan to reform the House. The Democratic Party leadership saw this as an attempt to circumvent the rules and an unwillingness to work within the party structure. The article served to isolate Kefauver from the leadership in his own party.[6]

Truman had always disliked Kefauver, famously calling him "Cowfever," even though the two men had similar backgrounds and had risen to the top of the Democratic Party as Southern supporters of Franklin Roosevelt and the New Deal. To Truman, Kefauver had shown that he had no real party loyalties, and Truman was, if nothing else, a loyal Democrat. Kefauver's wavering disloyalty was more than Truman could abide. Kefauver had also been responsible for ending the political career of Illinois Senator Scott Lucas, the Democratic Party's majority leader in the Senate. In 1950, Lucas was locked in a reelection battle for his Senate seat with Illinois conservative Everett Dirksen. Lucas asked Kefauver not to investigate a long-running Illinois police scandal until after the election. Kefauver refused. On the eve of the election, a number of news reports were released that damaged Lucas's campaign and he lost.[7] Dirksen soon became one of the leading lights of the Republican Right, the man who had defeated the Democratic Party's majority leader in the Senate. And again, Truman saw all this as an apostasy against the Democratic Party.

Kefauver also made it clear that he intended to launch a crusade against corruption in Washington. Truman saw this as a slap in his face, a direct reference to the corruption uncovered in his administration. And then, to add to the insults, Kefauver took his anticrime committee on the road, making a well-publicized stop in Kansas City, Truman's backyard. *Life* magazine, as early as February 1952, saw Truman's courting of Stevenson as little more than an attempt to undercut Kefauver's candidacy.[8]

By early April, Kefauver was finally being taken seriously by the national media. "Not long ago," wrote the Alsop brothers in an article in the *Washington Post*, "the professionals almost unanimously laughed off Kefauver's efforts." But when Kefauver embarrassed Truman in the New Hampshire primary in March and then did surprisingly well in a write-in campaign in the Minnesota primary later that month, it was widely seen as two embarrassing defeats for Truman. Those two defeats (among other things) pushed Truman out of the campaign by late March. Then on April 1, the day after Truman left the race, Kefauver beat Oklahoma Senator Robert Kerr in the Nebraska primary, which was also perceived as a loss for Truman. With Stevenson continually denying his interest in his party's candidacy, only three Democratic candidates were left standing: Vice President Alben Barkley, Georgia Senator Richard Russell, and Kefauver. The Alsops considered Barkley too old, and Russell too Southern. "Kefauver," they predicted, "will go to the convention with delegates from Tennessee, Wisconsin and New Hampshire, and almost certainly from Oregon and California. Also probably Washington, Maryland, Florida, and Nebraska." In the final analysis, however, the Alsops expected Stevenson to announce that he would run for reelection as governor of Illinois, but then accept the Democratic nomination for president.[9]

Another Democrat looking for the nomination was Senator Richard Russell of Georgia. He was one of those great lions of the Senate, a decision maker, a coalition builder, a leader with all the qualities and abilities to be President of the United States. He had come to the Senate in 1930 at age thirty-five, then the youngest member of the body. He had, in fact, already served a term as the governor of Georgia. By 1950, he was the most important figure in the Senate. In that year, following the defeat of Scott Lucas of Illinois (the Democratic Party's majority leader in the Senate) Russell's closest allies urged him to step into the leadership role. Most observers at the time assumed that he would accept the post, but he finally demurred, insisting that he was too out of line with the national party, admitting, in fact, that his Southern exposure did not fit well with the party's national agenda.[10]

Instead, he said, he wanted to maintain his freedom. He wanted to devise and act on his own opinions and not become the spokesman for his party in the Senate. Russell finally threw his considerable support to Arizona Senator Ernest McFarland. For the second position, majority whip, he gave a nod to a young Lyndon Johnson, the newly elected senator from Texas. When McFarland was defeated by Barry Goldwater in the 1952 elections, Johnson moved into the majority leader position, again with Russell's blessing and support. From there, Johnson (with continued support from Senator Russell) maneuvered himself to become one of the most influential figures in Washington. In 1952, at age fifty-four, Richard Russell was still a young man with a long political career ahead of him. If he was ever going to make a run for the White House, this was the year.[11]

But despite Russell's considerable abilities, he carried the heavy yoke of a southerner, an old-time segregationist who had difficulty maneuvering inside the Democratic Party coalitions that included the liberal leaders of organized labor and the pragmatic Northern big-city bosses, all of whom seemed interested in little more than a candidate's ultimate electability. And Russell understood that. In October 1951, he wrote to a prominent Texan, insisting that the up-coming Democratic convention would not nominate "any man from a Southern state. They fear the prejudices which exist in some quarters. . . . I would prefer," he added "that some other Democrat represent the South at the next National Convention."[12]

In the decade following the war, race had become a sensitive issue, one that threatened to divide the Democrats. In the 1948 campaign, Truman had changed the dynamic considerably by making a direct bid for black votes by supporting several civil rights initiatives. Generally, the strategy worked. The president received over 80 percent of the African American vote in 1948, and he may well have won the electoral votes of several states outside the South because of his support for civil rights issues.[13] Taking the advice of several of his most liberal advisors, Truman met with black leaders, spoke to black audiences in Harlem, and worked hard for the passage of a permanent FEPC to regulate the hiring of African American workers in the nation's factories. For many southerners, and for their representatives in Washington, however, Truman's support for civil rights meant a slippery slope toward desegregation, racial equality, and a diminished role for Southern whites in what they saw as their social, political, and economic structure. They had no interest in Truman's political expediency. To Southern politicians, his acquiescence to black America was the beginning of the end for the white-dominated South. Their response was the Dixiecrat revolt.

In 1952 many of the South's big guns were threatening to bolt again, or at least they were threatening to support one of their own for president against the Northern Democratic Party choice—like Stevenson. Georgia Governor Herman Talmadge said he was on board. He was joined by South Carolina Governor James Byrnes, Senator Harry Byrd of Virginia, Louisiana Senator Russell Long, and Mississippi Senator John Stennis. These were powerful men in 1952 politics, southerners with a significant following in the South, and if they decided to walk out of the Democratic National Convention and take the third-party route, their leader, almost certainly, would be Russell.

Southern Democrats also believed that if they could nominate one of their own (or at least carry to the convention a swell of popular support) that they might regain some of their lost influence within the Democratic Party. Southern voters had become a political necessity for the Democrats by keeping the Northern liberal wing of their party in power. By the postwar years, however, that place in the party seemed misdirected. Why should Southern conservatives continue to support the agenda of Northern liberals? The events that led to the Dixiecrat revolt in 1948 had been nearly spontaneous. But by 1952 Southern leaders had begun to see their causes as unique, and outside the increasingly liberal agenda of the Democratic Party.

As the 1952 campaign approached, Southern leaders began discussing the possibility of again running one of their own in the campaign—take the Southern white vote off the table—if Truman insisted on making a run that year. Whether or not Truman feared this threat is not clear. Four years earlier, however, at the 1948 Democratic convention, he began to back away from his civil rights convictions when the South threatened to bolt the convention. Here, in 1952, with the South again talking about a third-party path, Truman announced that his time in the White House was over, and he withdrew from the 1952 campaign. Truman's decision to withdraw sat well with Russell, and presumably with other southerners. Russell wrote to the newly elected governor of Oklahoma that the president's decision not to run "will prove beneficial to the Party and to the country."[14]

Russell was hardly a radical by any definition. His biographer, Gilbert C. Fite, has written that Russell was a fairly mainstream Democrat, except for his well-known stand against civil rights for African Americans. He had been an enthusiastic supporter of the New Deal, and even a supporter of many of Truman's Fair Deal programs. The liberal ADA, in its published judgments of Washington's lawmakers, considered him "right" on most issues.[15] If he could have found a willingness in his character to compromise on a few issues, he might have made a good presidential candidate.

By backing Russell's 1952 candidacy, southerners had several very good options. Obviously, if Russell won the nomination their power would increase considerably. If he was chosen as the vice presidential candidate the power of the South in the party would also increase. Russell, however, rejected this idea, insisting often that he was not running for the vice presidency.[16] But it was a fairly common notion that if he were offered the number-two spot on the ticket (certainly if Eisenhower chose to become a Democrat and won the party's nomination) that Russell would take it. Finally, perhaps, the most logical option was that Russell would take the delegate votes of the South to the convention, and in that fairly powerful position, force a number of Southern-influenced planks into the party's 1952 platform, or even orchestrate the writing of the platform. This was an unspoken aspiration, mostly because it was perceived as the consolation prize behind the first two options. But it was the most realistic plan, the one that might give white southerners the most leverage against the party's Northern liberal wing. By 1952, those Democratic liberals had come to see the future of civil rights, and they were on the road to rejecting the needs of the white South.

Civil rights may have been a deciding factor in all this, but several southerners also disliked Truman's stance on other issues that affected them, particularly the Tidelands issue. The Tidelands are the nation's offshore holdings, under the ocean somewhere beyond the low water limit of the tide and within the nation's territorial waters. Once a vast oil reserve was discovered in these Tideland regions along the Gulf of Mexico, the question became immediate: Who would administer the Tidelands and who would take the significant revenue from the oil and gas production there? The states insisted that they controlled the Tidelands, but in 1947, the Supreme Court concluded instead that the Tidelands were the purview of the federal government. Truman made it clear that he agreed with the decision, and he did little to change it, or even argue against it. For southerners, particularly those from the Gulf States, that placed the president in the wrong column. For them, and for their representatives in Washington, revenue from the Tidelands' oil production should go to the states. Just before the election, Eisenhower stepped in and promised that, if elected, he would work to have Tidelands jurisdiction returned to the states.[17]

Richard Russell announced on February 28, 1952 that he would be a candidate for president. "I am a Jeffersonian Democrat," he began his announcement—in much the same way other Southern candidates had begun their announcements to run outside the Democratic Party. I "believe in the greatest practicable degree of local self-government," and, he added, "the maintenance of the rights of the states . . . is our protection against that loss of individual rights and liberties which has always followed undue centralization of authority."[18] But Russell understood as a southerner, trying to run as a national candidate, that his chances were not good. *Time* wrote of Russell's chances: "He has about as much chance of being nominated as a boll weevil has of winning a popularity contest at a cotton planters' picnic."[19] Russell went on to add that he had no intention of running as a third-party candidate, or of seeking the vice presidency. To *Life* magazine, he was not just a candidate, but the face of a "rebellion against the [Democratic] party."[20]

Russell tried desperately to shake the sectional candidate label and push for the broader appeal of a national candidate. He made a two-week campaign swing through the West, stopping and speaking in sixteen states. He insisted often that he was not a sectional candidate, not a candidate of the South. "Unless," he wrote to author Jonathan Daniels, "my bitter opposition to such proposals as [the] FEPC can be considered sectional."[21] At the same time, Kefauver was successfully portraying himself as a national candidate, despite his Southern roots in East Tennessee.

Russell would make his strongest stand against Kefauver in Florida. Just south of Russell's home state of Georgia, Russell thought that Floridians had similar sensibilities. But he also liked the idea of being able to move easily and quickly between his home state and Florida. He was so confident of a victory in Florida that he suggested to Kefauver in early April that the winner of the Florida primary take *all* of the state's delegates to the convention. Kefauver, who was probably not so confident, did not respond to Russell's challenge.[22] Russell began his campaign in Gainesville in the last days of April, and over a whirlwind ten days, he delivered major speeches in Pensacola, Miami, Orlando, and Jacksonville.[23] His plan was to win big in Florida, and then springboard into other primaries, (particularly California, which was scheduled for June 3) and finally into the convention with a solid delegate count. He continued to insist that he had no interest in the vice presidency, or of being a Dixiecrat third-party candidate. With Truman out of the running, and Stevenson still insisting that he was not interested in the nomination, Russell's only opponent seemed to be Kefauver.

But Kefauver was much more concerned with a challenge from Florida Governor Fuller Warren. A year earlier, Kefauver's crime committee had charged that Warren had ties to organized crime in Chicago, and by most accounts, Warren was preparing to hit back in the Florida primary. Warren challenged Kefauver to two televised debates, but showed up at neither. During the second "debate" Kefauver spoke to Warren's empty chair, while answering a series of questions sent to him by Warren. About an hour later on that same evening, May 5, Kefauver met Russell for a televised debate that focused on an FEPC. Russell insisted that equal employment would be a national travesty; Kefauver accused Russell of intending to take the South out of the Democratic Party if he did not get his way.[24]

Russell had the support of Florida's most important political leaders. Senator Spence Holland supported him, and so did Warren. Russell won the Florida primary with 54 percent of the votes but his showing was not strong enough to push his campaign forward. In fact, Kefauver lost in Florida, but he gave a fairly strong showing that catapulted him into an impressive victory in Ohio on May 6. There he ran against former Senator Robert Bulkley, perceived as a stand-in for President Truman. For Russell to have had an effective victory in Florida, he needed to bury Kefauver.[25]

Following the Florida primary, Kefauver tried to convince Russell to agree to the yet-unwritten Democratic Party plank on civil rights, regardless of the convention's decision. "Such action," Kefauver wrote, "will place this urgent and important issue where it belongs, before the party as a whole." Kefauver added that he was willing to subscribe to just such a pledge.[26] Russell responded to the bait: "I am amazed at your proposal to accept whatever plank may be adopted."[27]

After the 1952 primary season, Russell lost much of his political influence, particularly within the Democratic Party. He withdrew from the campaign, and then refused to aid Stevenson. Many of Russell's constituents pushed him to get onto the campaign trail, to stump for the Democratic nominee. But Russell continued to refuse, arguing often that the South was in the bag for Stevenson anyway. Why should he work to win Southern votes for a candidate who was going to carry the South? To those who would insist that he jump on the Stevenson bandwagon, he often wrote the same thing: "I do not know of any place where my support would be of material aid."[28] But almost certainly, Russell avoided the Stevenson campaign because of Stevenson's stands on civil rights, his call for an end to the Senate filibuster, and his insistence that each state adopt an FEPC.[29]

In August, Russell went to Springfield, Illinois to meet with Stevenson. Almost certainly, Stevenson hoped to recruit Russell's assistance in the campaign—probably outside the South. But the meeting went badly. "I felt greatly heartened by his candidacy," Russell wrote to a friend. "However, even while I was there [Stevenson] was being subjected to terrific pressure by the ADA group. I had a long fight with some of them," he added. In another letter, he seemed to conclude his thoughts: "There have been some indications that he is tending to yield to those pressures."[30]

In 1956, Russell got behind Lyndon Johnson's short-lived campaign. Johnson, from Texas, had tried almost desperately to shake the Southern attachment that had sunk Russell's 1952 campaign and tried to sell himself as a westerner, with Western values that were different than the values held by the South. Russell encouraged Johnson's apparent shift in loyalties, due at least in part to his 1952 experience. When 101 Southern congressmen and senators signed the Southern Manifesto in 1956 as a protest to the Supreme Court's *Brown v. Board of Education* decision two years earlier, Russell counseled Johnson not to sign it. And even though it was probably Russell who conceived and wrote the document, he even protected Johnson from Southern criticism for not signing the Manifesto. Russell wanted Johnson to become president, and he knew that anyone who signed the Southern Manifesto would be responsible for alienating key voting sections of the nation outside the South.[31]

The only other primary that held significance for the Democrats was Nebraska, held on April 1. Kefauver faced an important challenge there from Robert Kerr, the Senator from Oklahoma. Kerr had made a fortune in the Oklahoma oil fields, and then in 1944 he played an important, behind-the-scenes role in Truman's vice presidential nomination. He won a Senate seat in 1948, and then began considering a run for the White House in 1952. But Kerr was a loyal Truman man, and he refused to announce his candidacy until Truman was well outside the political arena. He was finally persuaded to enter the Nebraska primary as a favorite son, a Truman surrogate who would hold the state's delegates for the president. Kefauver went on the attack, calling Kerr a mere "stand-in" for Truman, and not a real candidate. When Truman finally withdrew from the race, two days before the Nebraska vote, Kerr announced that he was an all-out candidate. But it was too late. Kefauver trounced Kerr in the final vote count.[32]

There were other Democrats. In fact, Drew Pearson wrote in his diary that "Washington is agog. Democratic candidates are everywhere."[33] It was one of those election years. No candidate really stood up; the incumbent was unpopular and wavered, and anyone who was any sort of leader in American Democratic Party politics decided that this was their year. Of the candidates who occupied the sidelines, hoping that electoral events would fall their way, Averell Harriman was probably the most prominent. Perhaps Harriman's greatest liability was that he was probably one of the richest men in America. He was the son of E. H. Harriman, the builder and president of the Union Pacific Railroad. Averell had, himself, built up a distinguished career as a public servant. And if personal wealth was a detriment in 1952, a nod from Truman was an advantage. Harriman was a genuine liberal, almost certainly the most liberal of all the potential Democratic candidates. He had been a die-hard supporter of New Deal and Fair Deal programs, and he seemed to see the future in the politics of civil rights. Truman's infatuation with Harriman only went as far as Stevenson's denials. And Truman made that pretty clear to Harriman.[34] At the convention, when Stevenson said yes, Truman abruptly turned his back on Harriman.

Democratic presidential candidates were everywhere in 1952. And if Stevenson continued to deny interest in the nomination, then Truman would continue fishing. He wanted to anoint a successor, even if it was Harriman or Barkley.

Chapter 6

The 1952 Campaign as the Beginning of the Future of American Politics

President Harry Truman was the last of the New Dealers. His Fair Deal programs grew out of Roosevelt's depression-era policies. Truman's plans and programs, however, had more to do with getting reelected than any need to solve the nation's economic problems. In fact, the economic problems faced by the nation in those years immediately following the war (overabundance and a fear of inflation) were the exact opposite of the problems that Roosevelt faced in the 1930s. Nevertheless, Truman's policies are still viewed as a direct extension of the New Deal. His successor in the Democratic Party, and the party's standard bearer in the next decade, was Illinois Governor Adlai Stevenson. Stevenson was no Truman, and he certainly was no Roosevelt. Many of his followers, however, hoped he would become the direct political successor of their beloved Roosevelt. He was urbane, witty, and even charming—many of the characteristics often attributed to Roosevelt. But he had no great desire to carry on the New Deal-Fair Deal legacy of the Democratic Party. In fact, it could be argued, by comparing statements and deeds over time, that Eisenhower may well have been more liberal (at least on some social issues) than Stevenson had ever been.

Stevenson came to believe that Truman (with a dismal approval rating below 30 percent) might, in fact, damage his campaign against Eisenhower in 1952. That may have been a mistake; Truman had considerable appeal to the common man, something that Stevenson truly lacked. At the same time, Truman wanted a successor, someone who would follow him in office, carry on the New Deal-Fair Deal tradition, and keep the Republicans out of Washington. Stevenson agreed to accept the nomination, but he rejected all of Truman's advances, and he even spurned the president's assistance on the campaign trail. He also wanted to rid himself of the albatross of corruption in the Truman administration, or "that mess in Washington," as events

61

in the last years of Truman's terms in office were often called. The result was a significant break in the history of the Democratic Party between the politics of the past and the politics of the future. Out went much of the old New Deal-Fair Deal Democratic tradition, and in came a new political tradition that better fit the times. Stevenson's new tack represented a more moderate, more business-friendly philosophy that pulled away from the paternalism and economic management of the previous decades. Stevenson was also inclined to support civil rights for African Americans. And if that meant losing Southern white votes, Stevenson was prepared to accept that. Truman had made a few gestures in that direction in 1948, and Stevenson might be called a "gradualist" on civil rights who often feared the political repercussions of a civil rights stance. But throughout his two campaigns, he was an outspoken supporter of the 1954 *Brown* decision and civil rights for African Americans.

Lyndon Johnson's moderation through the 1950s added to all this. He was the Democratic Party leader through the decade, even more so than Stevenson or even the Democratic National Committee chairman, Paul Butler. Johnson's moderation in the Senate set the stage for most of the Democratic Party's policies during the decade, as did Sam Rayburn's equally moderate leadership in the House of Representatives. Their moderation had as much to do with their relationship with Eisenhower and his popularity with voters as with their own convictions. The result was a moderate Democratic Party through the 1950s.[1] Lyndon Johnson's Great Society programs of the next decade have often been characterized as something of a divergence from that trend of 1950s-style moderation, a belated successor to the old depression-era Democratic liberal traditions. Certainly, Johnson, in the mid-1960s, wanted to be the new FDR, the president who brought an increased economic equality to the American people while winning a war against an international evil. He may even have wanted to fulfill what he believed to be the mandate that his party and the nation had given to John Kennedy in the 1960 election. To that end, he hoped to follow the old New Deal-Fair Deal tradition. But much of Johnson's Great Society programs failed, crushed under the weight of the cost of the programs themselves, and the president's own commitment to the war in Vietnam. Johnson's Great Society was truly the last gasp of the New Deal-style liberalism.[2] Because of this split between Truman and Stevenson in 1952 (and because of the deep-seated moderation of both Stevenson and Johnson) the decade of the 1950s remains one of the primary turning points in Democratic Party politics.

* * *

Eisenhower's policies in the 1950s caused a directional shift in the Republican Party that was also significant. Like Stevenson and Johnson, Eisenhower was a moderate. He was so moderate, in fact, that he often bandied about the word "liberal" to describe some of his own policies. Through his first administration this moderation brought very little pushback from the powerful right wing in his party. The president was extremely popular, and his coattails were long and predictable. To confront Eisenhower could mean losing an election. So, for a while, the Right pandered to Eisenhower. But that soon changed. The GOP Right grew stronger through the 1950s in opposition to Eisenhower's moderation. Their leadership was generally weak, but their numbers increased in Congress through the decade. In the 1960 campaign, Richard Nixon (by then reinvented as an Eisenhower moderate) lost to John Kennedy. The battle cry went up immediately. Nixon had lost because of his moderation, his "me-tooism." And the Republican Right re-emerged as a power. They nominated their darling, Barry Goldwater, and promptly lost the 1964 election to the Lyndon Johnson juggernaut. But Barry Goldwater's campaign paved the way for the growth of the Republican Right that eventually saw fruition in the nomination and election of Ronald Reagan in 1980. It was Eisenhower's moderation (and his workings with Lyndon Johnson and Democratic moderates through the 1950s) that alienated the GOP Right. And that, in turn, led to their growth and influence in the party—and eventually to the rise of the Republican Right and Reagan's election.[3]

By the end of the 1950s, the future of American politics was coming into focus. Both parties were undergoing major transformations. In addition to the rise of the Republican Right in opposition to Eisenhower's moderation, a new Republican Party geographic coalition was also forming. The conservative South was joining with Midwestern conservatives and generally rejecting the historically more moderate Northeastern wing of the party—surrendering that region to the Democrats. By 1964, with Barry Goldwater's run, that coalition would add much of the American West. The Republicans suffered an ignominious defeat that year, but by the next election cycle in 1968 the Southern-Midwestern-Far Western Republican coalition would be in place. Add to that the age-old traditional Republicans (a group almost always overlooked in the calculations of coalitions) and the increasing strength of the nation's growing suburbs, and a new Republican coalition was born. It was strong, and it would stay in place for the remainder of the century. When pollster Lou Harris asked in 1954, "Is There a Republican Majority?" the answer he gave was "yes." A new Republican majority, he seemed to be saying, was on the horizon.

The new coalition was much more conservative, and it would field conservative candidates clear into the next millennium. Prior to 1960 or so, Republican presidential candidates had been moderates, like New York Governor Tom Dewey. Eisenhower (always supported strongly by Dewey and his circle) and a short time later, Nelson Rockefeller, also fell into that group. Alf Landon and Wendell Willkie, both of whom lost presidential campaigns to Franklin Roosevelt, were also Republican moderates. By the mid-1960s, however, that wing of the party had been purged by the growing Republican Right. The moderates were often characterized as the purveyors of "me-tooism," the dreaded accusation inside the party that denoted a Republican who was so liberal that he supported most (or various aspects) of the New Deal-Fair Deal agenda. With the Northeastern moderates out, the new coalition focused on the issues of anticommunism, lowering taxes, and reducing the size of the federal government. By 1980, when Reagan ran and won with that coalition well defined and those issues firmly in hand, the Republican Party had achieved its transformation from Eisenhower moderation to Reagan conservatism. It was, by then, a more conservative (and a much stronger) party.

It was Eisenhower who first saw the future of the Republican Party in the South. Since Reconstruction, race and race issues had defined Southern politics. African Americans voted (when they were allowed to vote) Republican, the party of Lincoln, and Southern whites were generally Democrats. By the end of World War II, much of that began to change. The Democrats slowly took on the mantle of the party of civil rights, the party that would be the future for African American voters. If there was any question about the Democratic Party's growing support for civil rights, there was the 1948 Democratic convention during which the Democrats refused to give their support to the white Southern delegations when they insisted on their usual states' right clause in the party's platform. After a fight on the convention floor, Hubert Humphrey (the then mayor of Minneapolis and running for a Senate seat from Minnesota) called for the party to "get out of the shadow of states' rights and to walk forthrightly into the bright sunshine of human rights." And with that, the entire Mississippi delegation and part of the Alabama delegation walked out of the Philadelphia convention and formed the States' Rights Party, better known in history as the Dixiecrats. They nominated their own candidates for president (South Carolina's Strom Thurmond) and vice president (James Eastland from Mississippi).[4]

The final impact of the Dixiecrats on the 1948 election results was minimal. But the walk out marked the beginning of a trend that sent a large number of African American voters to the polls to cast their votes for Truman, the Democrat. The shift had begun. White southerners (always conservative) saw their future in the Republican Party, and the Democratic Party became the party of civil rights, or at least the party that made the most promises to African Americans. In 1952, Eisenhower saw this—in fact before most anyone. He saw that the Solid South was breakable, that there were Southern white votes to be had there. In fact, he may well have seen the future of his party in the South. Against the advice of his campaign staff, Eisenhower headed off to campaign in the South. It was the first time since Reconstruction that a Republican presidential candidate had bothered to campaign in the South for Southern white votes. Eisenhower's inroads into the white South in

1952 made no difference in his final victory over Stevenson, but both the 1948 and the 1952 elections set a strong foundation for the future. The process would be slow, but white southerners would find a home with the Republicans, and the nation's African Americans would eventually abandon the party of Lincoln and become Democrats.

In 1952, Eisenhower took Texas, Oklahoma, Missouri, Tennessee, Virginia, Maryland, Delaware, Kentucky, and Florida. Four years later, in 1956, he held onto most of those states, losing only Missouri, but adding Louisiana. Democrats always assumed that it had been Eisenhower's personal appeal that had brought white Southern voters to his side in 1952 and again in 1956. But Nixon's numbers in the 1960 campaign showed that the white South was actually in transition from the Solid South of the post-Reconstruction-era Democratic Party into the Republican Party—and that the transition was continuing, even picking up steam as the 1950s ended and the next decade began. Not only did Nixon, in 1960, increase voter strength throughout the South, he outran Eisenhower's 1956 numbers in four of the South's most Southern states: Alabama, Georgia, Mississippi, and South Carolina. Although he ultimately lost all of those states to Kennedy, he did win Virginia, Kentucky, Florida, Oklahoma, and Tennessee. And in a national losing effort, he maintained Eisenhower's 1956 strength in three of those states: Virginia, Florida, and Tennessee. Nationally, Nixon showed best in the rural regions of the nation, but in the South his support came from what was being touted as the New South, Southern cities like Atlanta, Birmingham, Dallas, and Houston—and the large and growing white suburbs that had begun springing up on the outskirts of those cities.[5]

In 1968, Nixon lost large parts of the South to George Wallace, then running as a third-party candidate. But in 1972, Nixon swept the South. Georgia Governor Jimmy Carter returned the South back to the Democrats briefly in 1976. But from 1980 until 1992, the South remained firmly in Republican hands. Arkansas Democrat Bill Clinton made some significant inroads back into the South in 1992 and again in 1996, but George W. Bush took all the South handily in 2000 and again in 2004. The vast majority of the South continued in the Republican column in 2008 and 2012.

As the 1950s came to a close, the Democrats had taken control of the industrial Northeast (generally abandoned by the Republicans), and they kept control of most of the nation's industrial regions. The Democrats had also won the votes of the nation's African Americans. Kennedy, in 1960, had really done little to appeal to black voters, but he did set up a civil rights division within his campaign structure and placed two very capable men there: Harris Wofford and Sargent Shriver. With little more than grinding hard work, Wofford and Shriver, at the head of groups of volunteers and campaign workers, put Kennedy's name before the nation's black community.

But it was Kennedy's dealing with Martin Luther King's arrest in Georgia in mid-October 1960 that allowed for a major shift in the black vote. Kennedy, right in the midst of the presidential campaign, called Mrs. King to console her immediately following her husband's arrest. Robert Kennedy, then, placed a call to the Georgia judge who had sent King to the Georgia State Penitentiary. That finally affected his release.[6] It became one of several great turning points in the postwar civil rights movement. And it was one of several events that pushed black voters out of the party of Lincoln and into the Democratic Party. That shift could be seen in national voting numbers, and not only in the South. Gallup reported that seven out of ten African Americans nationwide voted for Kennedy in 1960.[7] In 1956, 64 percent of New York City's African American population had voted for Stevenson. But in 1960, that number jumped to 74 percent. The numbers went from 63 to 78 percent among Chicago's African American voters. In Pittsburgh, the increase was from 68 to 78 percent; 48 to 74 percent in Baltimore, 36 to 64 percent in Atlanta, and 19 to 65 percent throughout the entire rural South.[8]

The black vote was important in establishing Democratic majorities in many large Northern urban areas, particularly New York, Chicago, Detroit, Pittsburgh, Cleveland, and several others. These votes were often instrumental in awarding to the Democrats the electoral totals of states that were much more conservative. Perhaps Michigan and Illinois are the best examples. Although both states had generally conservative white populations, they often tilted to the Democrats (at least in part) because of huge African American vote totals in those states' major cities. Some of this shift was apparent in the polls as early as 1948. In that election, Truman made several gestures toward African American voters and won the electoral votes of Illinois, California, and Ohio. Of course, it was not only black voters who pushed those states into the Democratic column; the labor vote, for instance, was equally important in Truman's victories in those industrial states. In addition, Truman missed winning the electoral votes of Pennsylvania, Indiana, and Michigan by less than one percent of the popular vote in each of those states. By the end of the 1950s—and then into the next decade, the Democrats maintained firm control of the black vote (both nationally and in the South). In addition, by 1960, the Democrats were pretty solid in most of the nation's industrial states like Pennsylvania, Michigan, and Illinois. Again, this electoral strength was at least due in part to the urban black vote.[9]

The Democratic Party's coalition after the 1950s is more difficult to define than the Republican Party coalition and their new geographic realignment. During and after the 1950s, the Democrats continued to rely on portions of the old New Deal coalition that had formed in the mid-1930s. They had managed to pull into their party structure African Americans, both North and South, at least in part because Northern whites had begun their move into the Republican Party in those years. They also continued to control the votes of groups like urban immigrants, voters in the lower income brackets, various minority groups, and organized labor in the industrial states and cities. However, through the next decades, the demographics of these groups changed considerably. The immigrants became second-generation Americans. People in the lower income brackets moved up into the middle classes; the ranks of organized labor decreased significantly, and whites in the cities began moving into the more conservative suburbs. The result was that many of these groups abandoned their Democratic Party-inspired liberalism for a more conservative view of the world, and the size of the Democratic Party began to shrink in both popularity and numbers. By the 1980s, that process was generally complete, and the Democrats found it difficult to maintain majorities at almost all levels of government. Pundits explained that the Democrats were resting on their laurels of the New Deal-Fair Deal programs (which blamed the Republicans for the 1930s economic depression and the narrowness of McCarthyism). By the 1980s those arguments no longer appealed to voters. The Democrats, the pundits insisted, needed new ideas and new leadership. All of these changes began in the 1950s.[10]

Another change in American politics in the 1950s was the greater significance that began to be placed on the personal image of political candidates, with the result that American politics would never be the same again. Political writers still want to explain how the 1960 campaign (when the attractive Kennedy beat the unattractive Nixon) was at the origins of a new age in political advertising, the first presidential campaign in which image trumped substance. But as with most aspects of the 1960s, that trend began in the 1950s. Eisenhower was well aware of his image. He had an infectious smile. He even had an appealing nickname. Add to that his hero status, his past accomplishments, his clean image, and even his place as something of an all-American symbol, and he became one of the most appealing political candidates of the twentieth century. His opponents had yet to realize the significance of image. Bob Taft may have, in fact, understood it, but he was never able to overcome his stiff image, and he was never able to portray himself as a man of the people, an image that he believed would bring him the Republican nomination. As early as the 1948 campaign, Taft had even gone so far as to hire a media consultant, something mostly unheard of in those years. The consulting firm he hired was headed by General Oscar Solbert (who had been chief of the nation's psychological warfare strategy during the war). The plan was to pump up Taft's image from a stale legislator to a bright, vibrant, electable political candidate with a forward-looking agenda. The result was the predictable campaign literature filled with the beaming smiles and the slap-on-the-back personal life of a very human figure: "Bob Taft is by no means an austere or aloof person," the literature stated.[11]

Eisenhower's Democratic adversary in both elections, Adlai Stevenson, refused to consider image control as an important part of his campaigns—much to his detriment. There were seventeen million television sets in the United States in 1952, and that medium was about to jump onto the American political scene. But Stevenson did not watch television, and he never really understood it, or its potential impact on politics. It was Lyndon Johnson, however, who even more so represented the anti-image personality in the 1950s. Johnson was not an attractive man; he did not have an infectious smile, and, in fact, if he represented anything it was the American South—an image that he tried to brush off through most of his career by proclaiming himself a westerner from Texas and not a southerner. His greatest talent was his ability to maneuver the Senate, to build coalitions, and get legislation passed. Somehow, Johnson believed that ability would make him an appealing figure to American voters. And several times throughout his career, he seemed to want to do little more than point to his accomplishments and present to the nation's voters his resume' of congressional victories. Most Americans, however (if they knew of Johnson at all), saw him as a political wheeler-dealer whose primary ability was to weaken liberal legislation. As vice presidential candidate in 1960, and then as vice president in the Kennedy administration, the Kennedys (family, friends, and advisors) referred to him as "colonel cornpone." Even as president, Johnson was unable to shake that terrible image. Only in the 1964 presidential campaign did he take the advice of others (from people around him like Bill Moyers) that a campaign to destroy your opponent's image might be as successful as building your own.[12] In the 1950s, however, Lyndon Johnson knew little or nothing of the significance of image in American politics.

But Eisenhower did understand. His use of television and campaign ads helped him win in 1952. Then in 1956, he ramped up his advertising operation (mostly in an effort to use media ads in place of personal campaigning) and buried Stevenson in both the polls and in the quality and quantity of on-air advertising. In the next campaign, in 1960, Kennedy came to realize that he would have to engage in heavy advertising in order to beat Nixon.[13]

American politics at the end of the 1950s was considerably different than it had been at the beginning of the decade. The New Deal-Fair Deal era was at an end, even though large numbers of Democratic loyalists continued to long for the years of Franklin Roosevelt, New Deal liberalism, and a tradition in the party of economic planning and problem solving. The Republican Party had realigned, recalculated its conservatism, and reached a genuine parity with the Democrats. But they had also begun a debilitating split between the Eisenhower moderates and the GOP Right that would have repercussions for decades to come. The decade of the 1950s is often perceived as a time of holding the line, of maintaining the *status quo*, but in American politics, the nation was in the process of making great changes that would last for decades to come.

Chapter 7

Conventions

Both parties headed off to their respective Chicago conventions without concrete decisions as to who their candidates would be. Since the 1970s, the two parties have chosen their candidates through national primary campaigns that have lasted most of the election year cycle. But in the immediate postwar years, primaries only played a small part in the nominating process. Often parties would assemble at their conventions without a certain candidate in place, and the delegates would fight it out, voting, and voting again, until one candidate emerged, collected the number of delegate votes needed, and accepted the nomination of the party. Such was the case with both party conventions in 1952.

If there ever was a city that fit the bill as a national convention city, it was Chicago. It was centrally located. It had the facilities for a convention, all located near downtown. And Chicago could claim the experience to do the job. Four years earlier, in 1948, both parties had made (what was considered by many) the terrible choice of moving their conventions to Philadelphia, where it was hot, rainy, and both parties had a fairly awful experience: Tom Dewey had been nominated by the GOP in an air of perceived victory, and then lost the election; and the Democrats had nominated Truman in an atmosphere of defeat, leading the South to bolt the party to run their own third-party candidate. The Chicago Convention Building and International Amphitheater (although a couple of miles from the downtown Loop) boasted a new air-conditioning system, and it had several advantages to accommodate the new medium of television. The Republican convention was set to open on July 7. By that time, by most accounts, Taft was within striking distance of a first ballot victory over Eisenhower. But when the Republican delegates arrived at their hotels in Chicago, they were hit immediately with the Fair Play Resolution, a challenge being pushed by Eisenhower's people. Some state delegations had come to Chicago contested. Delegates from eight states (as many as seventy-five delegates) had filed complaints with the Republican National Committee that their validity was somehow in question. The most important of that group was Texas, with thirty-eight contested delegates. Eisenhower's supporters had drafted a telegram that accused the Truman administration of corruption in office, and insisting that in order for the Republican Party to combat that corruption, "the Republican nominee [must] enter the campaign with clean hands, and no question can be raised regarding the methods employed in his securing the nomination."[1] It was Taft's people who controlled the RNC and the other committees that would decide the issue, and it looked as though Taft (and not Eisenhower) would win the contested delegate decisions. But Taft's people insisted that the decisions regarding the contested delegates be made behind closed doors, not televised, and without the presence of the press. That decision, apparently, made the press people covering the convention mad, and Taft began to be treated badly in the press.[2] Within just twenty-four hours, Taft went from a legitimate presidential candidate to a heavy-handed villain who, it seemed, would do just about anything necessary to steamroll the nomination. The issue, then, shifted from who would control the contested delegates to personal image, a fight that Taft had never been able to win. Eisenhower appeared to be the underdog, about to be trampled by the Taft juggernaut. Taft saw his image weakening (and Eisenhower's growing) over a few contested delegates that really held little significance in the greater scheme of the total delegate count.[3] In an attempt to defuse the situation, Taft sent word that he would compromise on the issue and agree to divide the delegates. "While I will suffer a delegate loss in making this proposal," Taft said in an almost surrender of the entire issue, "I am doing so because I think it is so generous that its equity cannot be questioned."[4] But Eisenhower's people, particularly Henry Cabot Lodge, knew the value of a moral victory and rejected Taft's compromise. The Republican National Committee, then, accepted Taft's overtures and divided the Texas delegation.[5] Lodge, however, refused to surrender the moral victory, and announced that he would take the fight to the convention floor.[6] There the vote against Taft (and in support of Fair Play) was unanimous. Taft was beaten.

By the end of the first day, the Republican delegates had fought the Fair Play fight, and it was pretty clear that Eisenhower would win the nomination. It was time for the keynote speech, probably the most anticipated speech of the convention besides the acceptance speech of the candidate himself. Chosen for the speech was Douglas MacArthur, the man who orchestrated the defeat of Japan. And in Korea, it was assumed by most Republicans that the North Koreans and the Chinese were about to be defeated when Truman decided to fight a limited regional war rather than accept MacArthur's advice and attack China (and perhaps even the Soviet Union). Because of the disagreement, Truman had felt a need to fire MacArthur. Who better to fire up the Republican base? But by the time MacArthur took to the podium, the wars of the Republican convention had been won and lost, and MacArthur appeared on the losing side. His speech was long, long-winded, and rambling. He had wanted the nomination himself. Save that, he had hoped to be chosen as Taft's running mate. But by the end of the first day, neither of those prospects were possible. MacArthur knew it, and the delegates knew it. He droned on for an hour on the inadequacies of the Truman administration, its weaknesses and the lack of leadership in Korea. The delegates cheered. But MacArthur's time had come and gone. *The New York Times'* headline confirmed that "MacArthur Role Fades," and the last line of the article by veteran war correspondent, Anne O'Hare McCormick, was that "MacArthur's keynote address [was] out of tune and out of context with the debate that preceded it."[7]

Following MacArthur, Illinois Senator Everett Dirksen spoke on behalf of his friend and fellow conservative, Bob Taft. But Dirksen was more interested in hitting hard at the moderate wing of his party. He singled out Tom Dewey, who was sitting on the floor with his New York delegation. Pointing an accusatory finger directly at Dewey, Dirksen brought down the House directly onto the 1944 and 1948 losing candidate. "We followed you before and you took us down the road to defeat." Then he warned, with a clear reference to Dewey's support of Eisenhower. "And don't do this to us again."[8] The next day, however, Joe McCarthy spoke to the same crowd and woke things up. By some accounts, McCarthy had bullied his way on to the convention program. But McCarthy was up for reelection. Taft's people controlled the committee that chose the speakers. They chose McCarthy because they wanted him to deliver a major address that placed a spotlight directly on the Communist menace. Eisenhower's people were clearly stunned by the choice, but the Republican Right (personified by McCarthy and Taft) would have their say—and they would have a place on the ticket if Eisenhower won the nomination.[9]

McCarthy began his speech by insisting that he would not soften his blows on the Communist issue because, he said, "a rough fight is the only fight Communists can understand." He received a four-minute ovation, along with a music display of "On Wisconsin," the fight song of the University of Wisconsin, ignoring the fact that McCarthy had graduated from Marquette University. The core of his speech resonated with the GOP's Far Right Wing, the anti-Communist wing of the Republican Party. The moderates in the party, however, sat on their hands. McCarthy "shouted," as *The New York Times* wrote: "I say, one Communist in a defense plant is one Communist too many. One Communist on the faculty of one university is one Communist too many. One Communist among the American advisors at Yalta was one Communist too many."

This last statement with a strong emphasis on the word "was" was a clear reference to Alger Hiss, one of Roosevelt's primary advisors at the Yalta Conference in February 1945, the big betrayal (as the Republican Right saw it) of the Roosevelt administration that turned over Eastern Europe to Soviet communism, and "enslaved," through forced occupation, as many as 100 million people.[10] Then he added, "And even if there were only one Communist in the State Department, that would still be one Communist too many."[11] The speech hit the mark with the delegates. They cheered and yelled approvingly as McCarthy seemed to touch every nerve. *The New York Times*, however, responded that McCarthy's speech had caused the convention to hit "rock bottom."[12] And President Truman called the speech "a damned lie."[13]

On the first ballot vote, taken on July 10, Eisenhower got within nine votes of the 604 needed to win the nomination. With that, Harold Stassen, a minor candidate who controlled twenty-eight delegates, released his delegates and that put Eisenhower over the top. Others followed, and the push for Eisenhower became a landslide.[14] Ohio Senator John Bricker, speaking for Taft, approached the podium and urged the convention to make the nomination of Eisenhower unanimous. The convention roared its approval. It was the third time Bricker had withdrawn the name of his good friend, Robert Taft, from contention. It would be the last. The decades-old adage that "Taft can't win" had, apparently, come true. Taft said he would not run again, and that three times was enough.[15] Later he blamed the New York financial interests and "a large number of businessmen subject to New York influence" for his defeat. He added that "four-fifths of the influential newspapers in the country were opposed to me vociferously and many turned themselves into propaganda sheets for my opponent." The press, he added, was "completely unfair in their treatment of [his candidacy]."[16] In a show of party unity, Eisenhower made the walk up Michigan Avenue, across Balbo Drive from his hotel, the Blackstone, to Taft's campaign headquarters in the Hilton. James Hagerty, who accompanied Eisenhower, recalled later that "there were a lot of Taft people in tears. It was a dramatic scene. And Bob was pretty choked up himself." But Hagerty saw it for what it was "the start of the healing of the internal wounds of the Party."[17] Eisenhower and Taft would meet again in an effort to shore up their differences. The next question to be answered was who would be Eisenhower's running mate? MacArthur believed that he was about to be offered the second spot, apparently not seeing the problem of two World War II generals on the same ticket, neither with any political experience. Dirksen's name was bantered around as the politically experienced domestic lawmaker who would offset Eisenhower's superior foreign policy credentials. But Dirksen had put off party moderates with his impetuous finger-pointing convention speech that blamed Dewey for the party's past woes. Taft was, himself, a choice by several Eisenhower insiders as a strategy that might be used to heal the party's wounds.[18] Eisenhower, at the same time, had little input (or interest) in the decision; he seemed to want to leave that to the politicians, the people who knew more about the pairing of candidates than anyone. By some accounts, Nixon had been offered the spot as early as May, perhaps by Dewey or Lodge, or both.[19] The final decision was made in a smoke-filled room at the Chicago Hilton. There, all the party big wigs made the decision, including Hagerty, Dewey, Brownell, Duff, Adams, Colorado Governor Dan Thornton, and RNC Chairman Arthur Summerfield. As Hagerty recalled, the group called Eisenhower to tell him that they had decided on Nixon. His response was clear: "Yes, fine."[20] And that was it. Nixon was on the ticket.

Of course, Nixon was a good choice, and not much of a surprise. As Herbert Brownell recalled,

> Eisenhower was old for a candidate, Nixon was young; Eisenhower had never had any experience in Congress, Nixon was an influential senator; Eisenhower . . . was considered an easterner and Nixon had a very strong political following in the west. . . . [A]nd Nixon had gained a national reputation in connection with the Hiss case and general opposition to communism in government ranks. . . . So it was a natural in that sense, [a] complimentary ticket[,] meeting . . . all the right requirements.[21]

Also, Nixon was from California, a state with a large electoral count. He had defeated Helen Gahagan Douglas, a popular liberal, in 1950 by more than 680,000 votes. And before that, he had defeated Democrat Jerry Voorhis for a House seat by 15,000 votes. But there may have been another reason that Nixon was so appealing to Eisenhower. The choice of Nixon buffered Eisenhower from any charges from McCarthy. McCarthy had hit hard at George Marshall for his supposed Communist sympathies in his book, *America's Retreat from Victory*, published the year before the presidential campaign. Certainly, Eisenhower hoped to avoid McCarthy's wrath, and the choice of Nixon as a running mate might keep McCarthy's attacks on Eisenhower (and Eisenhower's people) to a minimum.[22]

Nixon certainly thought more of Eisenhower than Eisenhower thought of Nixon. Late in 1951, while Eisenhower was still at SHAPE in France and contemplating a run for the presidency, Nixon visited Eisenhower. In his memoirs, Nixon wrote, "I felt that I was in the presence of a genuine statesman, and I came away convinced that he should be the next President. I also decided that if he ran for the nomination, I would do everything I could to help him get it."[23] For Eisenhower, running with Nixon was an expedient, a political decision designed to keep the party's right wing in line. Through Eisenhower's two administrations, he considered cutting Nixon from the ticket several times. By most accounts, however, Eisenhower "liked" Nixon, mostly the way a field general "likes" one of his loyal subordinates.[24]

At the same time, Eisenhower wanted to stay above the political infighting. He would take the high road and let Nixon do the dirty work of attacking the opposition. Throughout his life, Nixon had been called an "attack dog." And in the 1952 campaign, he would fill that bill. He attacked Stevenson as Truman's "hand-picked candidate"; as the candidate supported by Jack Kroll, the head of the CIO's political action committee; and of Chicago boss Jake Arvey.[25] He tried to connect Stevenson to Wilson Wyatt, one of the leading figures in the liberal Americans for Democratic Action.[26] He also continued to reference "that mess in Washington," a mess, he said, that was caused by the Democrats, and one that Eisenhower would clean up.[27] He attacked Sparkman for opposing civil rights for African Americans in the South, and he liked to call Stevenson "side-saddle Adlai" for his ownership of horses.[28] He often compared Stevenson to Dean Acheson, Truman's secretary of state, and what he referred to as the "wishy-washy State Department." "Mr. Stevenson," Nixon told a crowd in Boston, "has offered the American people nothing more constructive than a dreary continuance of the negative policy of containment. . . . To me this smacks unpleasantly of 1938 and 1939 when another dictator was temporarily appeased by the world's greatest give-away program."[29]

* * *

But it was the Democrats who had the biggest problems in 1952. Kefauver was ahead in the delegate count as the conventioneers arrived in Chicago in mid-July. He had been successful in several primaries, often running unopposed. He was perceived as a battler, a proven vote-getter, and he had a favorable reputation and strong party support among several important party figures and groups. He also had name recognition—a distinct advantage in an age before saturation news coverage. But Kefauver had problems. Most importantly, Truman did not like him. In fact, writing in one of his famous unsent letters, Truman called Kefauver "a demagogic dumb bell," unethical, and intellectually dishonest.[30] Kefauver had jumped into the race for the Democratic nomination before Truman had decided he would not run, and Kefauver had embarrassed Truman by beating him in the New Hampshire primary in March. When the dust finally cleared in Chicago, it would be Truman who would wield the most weight in the decision-making process, and Kefauver would find himself pushed aside. Kefauver was also not a favorite of the South (because of his record and statements on civil rights for African Americans), and the several Southern delegates were considering bolting the convention again, as they had four years earlier, if Kefauver won the nomination, and they did not get their way on civil rights.

Stevenson continued to insist that he was not interested in the nomination. As late as July 4, just eighteen days before the convention met, he sent out a statement declaring, "I utterly and emphatically deny specifying to newspaper men, political leaders, or anyone else, conditions under which I would accept the nomination."[31] A few days later, he sent a note to Walter Johnson, the leader of a draft-Stevenson movement, that he was "very much disturbed" at Johnson's committee for continuing to promote his candidacy.[32] Then on July 20, the day before the convention began, Stevenson complained in the *Chicago Tribune* that a Stevenson-for-president headquarters had been opened in Chicago "without my knowledge, approval, or acquiescence."[33] On that day, he complained to his own Illinois delegation: "I do not dream myself fit for the job—temperamentally, mentally, or physically. And I ask therefore that you all abide by my wishes not to nominate me, nor to vote for me if I should be nominated."[34] The draft-Stevenson movement, led by Johnson, immediately issued a statement that Stevenson would accept a draft: "Governor Stevenson, in view of his distinguished record of public service, would not reject a genuine desire on the part of the nation to ask him to continue such service at the highest level."[35] Two days later, on July 22, the day after the convention began, *The New York Times* called Stevenson a "reluctant" candidate.[36] The delegates at the Democratic convention, however, refused to accept his reluctance.

* * *

Television played a major role in the nominating decision, perhaps, for the first time, in 1952. There had been television cameras at the 1948 conventions, and about one million sets were tuned in to the event. But four years later, in 1952, it was projected that tens of millions of viewers would watch the two conventions.[37] Television was more important to the Democrats that year than the Republicans. The Republican candidates (Eisenhower and Taft) were fairly well known to the American public. But not so for the Democrats. Most Americans knew little of Adlai Stevenson, or most of the others running. Kefauver had been in the public eye for some time, but even he was not nearly as well recognized as Eisenhower.

To make certain that the viewing public saw their candidates, the Democratic National Committee erected several television cameras (very large box-like objects) directly in front of the speakers' podium. The cameras were so large that they nearly obstructed the audience's direct view of the speakers. But they did what they were intended: they allowed for close-up shots of the speakers, and that included the unfamiliar faces of the party candidates. The Republicans also chose to broadcast the actions of their convention, but only from the back of the auditorium.[38]

As usual, civil rights for African Americans was the Democratic Party's biggest problem, one it had grappled with at least since Reconstruction. In 1948 much of the South had walked out of the Philadelphia convention, and split the party badly. If it happened again in 1952, the outcome would almost certainly be devastating to the Democrats. Conservative white southerners had begun to make their way into the Republican Party, abandoning their long-time affiliation with the Democrats. There was no certainty that the Solid South would remain Democratic if the Southern delegations again walked out of the convention in 1952.

All party conventions are designed to excite the faithful, bring out patriotism, and present an air of victory and unity. But to the careful observer, conventions often present something completely different. Perhaps the convention presents an atmosphere of going-through-the motions in an air of impending defeat; or there is an underpinning of division; or simply there is the excitement for a new face. In 1952, the Democrats assembled with all the pageantry and excitement that goes with a political convention, but they had no strong candidate, no successor to the New Deal-Fair Deal tradition. Plus, they were divided badly, and the Truman administration had really not given the party anything to run on since his incredible 1948 victory. So, they fell back on their laurels. As *Time* reported in the days after the convention, "At times it seemed as if the Democrats had nothing to cheer but cheer itself." Their almost unanimous party line, it seemed, focused on what their party had accomplished twenty years ago. They argued that if the Republicans won the election they might take away all that the Democratic Party had accomplished. It was also clear that they no longer had the candidates capable of repairing the North-South rift, or the significant damage caused by the Truman administration. An article in *Time* added that the Democrats were looking, nearly in vain, for someone who could "put the party back where it was when Franklin Roosevelt died."[39]

But the Democrats did have a declared candidate. On July 6, Alben Barkley, Truman's vice president, announced that he would unabashedly seek the office.[40] And by some accounts, Barkley immediately jumped into the lead in the polls when Stevenson made a point several times of insisting that he would not allow the convention to draft him.[41] But at seventy-four, Barkley was considered too old for the job—in fact, much too old for the job. On Monday morning, July 21, the day the convention opened, Barkley invited several labor leaders to a friendly breakfast at the Conrad Hilton Hotel on Michigan Avenue in downtown Chicago. Those attending included Walter Reuther of the United Auto Workers, and Jack Kroll of labor's most active political action committee, the CIO-PAC. They let Barkley down as gently as they could. He was simply too old to win the nomination and too old to win the election. Truman (who was not yet in Chicago) had given some tentative support to Barkley, but once the labor leaders wavered, Truman abandoned his vice president, and Barkley withdrew his name from contention. Labor had their man by then. So did Truman. It would be Stevenson. Barkley had to go.[42] A distraught Barkley said the next day that it was labor that had broken his candidacy.[43] To most Democrats, however, Barkley's many years as a party leader deserved some recognition. On Wednesday, Barkley was allowed to address the convention. To those in attendance, his address was to be a heartfelt goodbye to one of the party's old pols. But Barkley took advantage of the situation and delivered a rousing campaign speech, accusing "certain self-appointed labor leaders" of pulling the plug on his candidacy. By most accounts, he spoke without notes, and mostly from the heart. His speech lasted nearly forty minutes and was followed by a thirty-minute demonstration. But his career was over.[44] Labor's shift away from Barkley was the first of several moves that eventually gave Stevenson the nomination.

As governor of the host state, it was Stevenson's place to welcome the delegates to Illinois. But Stevenson took the opportunity to deliver what most saw as a genuine, all-out campaign speech. James Reston of *The New York Times* wrote that Stevenson, "the reluctant candidate [had] talked himself right into the leading candidate's role." He "did not sound like a man who was merely trying to be a good . . . host."[45] Truman, still in Washington, also apparently approved of the speech. A *New York Times* reporter wrote that Truman saw it as "a fighting campaign talk, the sort he has long wanted from the reluctant man that so many Democrats wish to draft as their standard bearer."[46] And Stevenson's own sister, Buffie Ives, told the *Chicago Sun-Times* that she believed her brother would accept the nomination. In fact, her response was "of course Adlai will accept."[47] For just about everyone watching the events in Chicago, Stevenson was in the running—reluctantly, perhaps, but running.

In the wee hours of Tuesday morning, July 22, Kefauver's supporters pushed through the convention a resolution that required all states to sign a loyalty oath stating that their delegates would support the party's eventual nominee.[48] This immediately placed Southern delegates in a bind, and it was intended to do just that. The South (or at least parts of the South) had left the party in 1948 and formed the Dixiecrats. In 1952, many southerners were teetering, undecided about their place in the party. Would they stay, or would they go? A loyalty oath that would force them to support Kefauver (or worse, some Northern anti-segregationist candidate like Stevenson) might just push the Southern delegates out of the convention and into another Dixiecrat movement. Kefauver, even though he was from Tennessee, had little support among the Southern delegations. The South, in fact, was mostly wrapped around the candidacy of Richard Russell. A 1948-type bolt by southerners would certainly help Kefauver's nomination prospects. Southerners protested the loyalty-oath scheme vigorously, but later that same Tuesday, it appeared that Kefauver's plan had worked. Most of the Southern state delegations had signed the loyalty oath. But three refused: Louisiana, South Carolina, and Virginia. The South was in a rebellious mood again. In a caucus of Southern delegates the night before, it was decided that those three states would leave the convention (or perhaps be kicked out) and the rest of the South would follow in protest. Kefauver, it seemed, was moving closer to the nomination.

Sam Rayburn, however, was the convention's permanent chairman, and he had little use for Kefauver. He respected Truman, and he was certainly no Dixiecrat. Kefauver's loyalty-oath scheme was about to meet its match. Early on July 24, Thursday, Rayburn simply announced that all the Southern delegations would be seated. And the plan died.[49] Arthur Krock writing for *The New York Times* called it "a Halloween bogyman that frightened only its fabricators." In another article in the same issue, Krock wrote that the "fragments of the [loyalty] resolution were [resigned] to the ash can."[50]

On that same day, July 24, the convention adopted the party platform—in the past the focus of the party's deepest internal conflicts. Just about everyone expected fireworks and walkouts, but the South had made it plain that it would go along with the platform as long as it did not include an explicit call for an FEPC or the desegregation of the South's school systems. With that, the party platform was intentionally vague on the always-divisive issue of civil rights, and it was adopted with a quick voice vote.[51] The possibility of a walkout by the Southern delegation was averted, first by the collapse of the loyalty-oath scheme, and then by the acceptance of a moderate civil rights plank in the party platform. All this aided Stevenson's nomination by making him the anti-Kefauver candidate. He was now the candidate who opposed the loyalty-oath scheme, and the candidate who opposed purging the party of the South. The delegates began to rally around him.

The first ballot was really no surprise. Kefauver got 340 votes, Stevenson got 273, Richard Russell got 268, and Averell Harriman got 123 votes. The magic number, the number of votes needed to cinch the nomination was 616. No candidate was even close.[52] Following the first ballot, Truman (who had been sick with a severe respiratory ailment and a fever) headed for Chicago—presumably to break the deadlock.[53] The second ballot was also of little consequence, but Stevenson was beginning to show growing strength. Kefauver got 362. Stevenson moved up with 324 votes. Russell received 294. And Harriman got 121. Following the second ballot, Truman arrived. There were rumors that the president was about to throw his considerable support to Harriman, but instead he told Harriman that he would support Stevenson. Harriman realized that he could not win, and he responded by releasing his delegates and jumping on the Stevenson bandwagon. By most accounts, that broke the stalemate. Kefauver hoped he could throw his support to Stevenson and then be awarded the second place on the ticket. But Sam Rayburn continued to control the podium, and he refused to recognize Kefauver. The third ballot was close, but Utah (at the very end of the alphabetical listing) went over to Stevenson at the last minute and put Stevenson over the top with 617 votes, giving him the nomination.

Eben Ayers, an assistant press secretary to President Truman, kept a unique and detailed diary of his times in the White House. Ayers had an extensive and exclusive view of the 1952 Democratic Party convention, and his diary entry in the days before the convention gives insight into what was about to happen. To observers like Ayers, Stevenson's nomination was just a matter of time. "[T]he field is wide open for nearly a score of candidates," he wrote. He gave the names of the various players: Kefauver, Barkley, Russell, Robert Kerr, and Harriman. "In the background," he added, "is Governor Adlai Stevenson of Illinois, who seems the strongest [candidate] but now continues to declare he is not a candidate. It is my prediction that, in the end, it will be Stevenson."[54]

So, the question was immediate. Who would be Stevenson's running mate? Kefauver, as the second highest delegate vote-getter, was the lead choice. He was a southerner (albeit one disliked by most Southern politicians). He had strong name recognition. He was perceived as a battler, a fighter. He had a fairly good reputation, and major sections of the party supported him. But Truman had no place for Kefauver, and by the time Stevenson was nominated, Truman held the sway of the convention. Kefauver was out. That placed Russell in the lead. He was often depicted as actually running for the vice presidency. In fact, *Time* speculated on that possibility several months before.[55] And he seemed a good choice. He had name recognition. He would certainly keep the South in place. But Russell simply refused. "I [have] been independent too long now to accept any position that would commit me to policies that were the brainchild of any man."[56] Truman recorded in his memoirs that he, Stevenson, Rayburn, and DNC Chairman Frank McKinney met to decide who the vice presidential nominee would be. To that group, there was no one better than John Sparkman, Senator from Alabama.[57] He was a good choice. He offset Stevenson's Northern-ness, and he had a liberal voting record that was satisfactory to Northern liberals. As a southerner, he kept the Southern rebellion in line, but at the same time he had a moderate reputation on civil rights issues. His only real deficit was that he lacked name recognition, perhaps Stevenson's own big hurdle in his effort to run against the popular Eisenhower.

The two slates were set. Eisenhower, the moderate war hero was paired with Nixon, the "attack dog" and Communist hunter who represented the party's right wing. The Democrats had chosen Stevenson, the reluctant Illinois governor with a progressive record, a patrician's pedigree, and a Northern sensibility. He was paired with John Sparkman, a Southern senator with a moderate-to-liberal voting record. Sparkman was not a Dixiecrat, but he was also not sympathetic to the burgeoning civil rights movement. The Democratic ticket was designed to win over Northern liberals while keeping the conservative white South in line. The Republican ticket was intended to bridge the growing gap between the moderate and conservative wings of the party. The key word for the period was "balance." And both parties would take their balanced tickets into the campaign.

Chapter 8

The Campaign

The two main slogans of the campaign were almost predictable. For Eisenhower and the Republicans it was: "It's time for a change." Stevenson and the Democrats warned the electorate, "Don't let them take it away." Republican leaders also used K^1C^2, an easy-to-remember acronym that stood for Korea, Communism, and Corruption—the three issues that Republicans hoped to pin on the Democrats and drive home during the campaign.[1]

As the two campaigns got underway, it was clear that they had nearly opposite problems. The Republicans needed to heal their wounds and bring their divided party back together. Stevenson needed to separate himself from Truman, and push his candidacy as far away from the president as possible.

Stevenson also had the problem of running a campaign against one of the most famous men in the nation—in fact, in the world. James Reston wrote in *The New York Times*, in the days just after the Democratic National Convention in Chicago, that Stevenson "is running against a general known as Ike and whose face is as familiar as Uncle Sam's, but [Stevenson] could walk from Lake Michigan to Oak Park, a Chicago suburb, without ever being recognized."[2] Stevenson also had very little organization and very little money. Again, Reston observed: "He is still recovering from the shock [of being nominated]. But conceding the sincerity of his resistance to the nomination. . . . He did not plan a thing before the moment of his acceptance. . . . He did not hire a soul or promise a job."[3]

Eisenhower also had big problems. He had alienated the Taft wing of his party at the convention. And he needed Taft. Taft could bring the GOP Right back on board the Eisenhower campaign. He could also hold the Midwestern states, an area of the country where Stevenson was perceived as strong. To that end, Eisenhower sent Taft a message just after the convention.[4]

Eisenhower also let the nation know that he wanted to meet Taft—certainly a means of pressure on Taft who was not particularly excited about patching his differences with Eisenhower. In a speech in Cleveland, Eisenhower made it clear that he was not the obstacle to any such meeting. "I tell you," he told a crowd, "I look forward to meeting Senator Taft soon, and I have every reason to believe that he and I are going to form a real team to stand together in every corner of these United States."[5]

Taft was on vacation in Quebec when he received Eisenhower's invitation. He should, certainly, have expected the request. There was no question that a united party was a necessary formula for victory in November, and a divided party was just as certain for defeat. But Taft sat, for at least a month, before he responded. He was understandably reticent. Republican Party operative (and Taft's campaign manager for the East Coast) John D. M. Hamilton told Taft that "before you agree to [meet with Eisenhower] you should be informed [of] Eisenhower's viewpoints on the issues which are of paramount importance to your followers."[6] Taft's greatest fear was that Eisenhower was much too liberal, and, as he told Idaho Senator Herman Welker, "We may get another New Deal administration which will be a good deal harder to fight than the Democrats."[7]

Taft wrote to Everett Dirksen that he was "concerned about the result of such a meeting. I don't want it used to prove that I have now been converted to the General's principles." Then he added, "I don't want it made to look as if I were abandoning the principles for which I have campaigned, or abandoning my friends to the purge that so many Eisenhower supporters seem to [be planning] for them." Taft then asked Dirksen to approach Eisenhower first, and discuss his demands.[8]

Taft and Eisenhower finally met on September 12, at Eisenhower's home at Morningside Heights, just off Columbia University's campus on the Upper West Side of Manhattan. Following the meeting, Taft told reporters that he and Eisenhower had reached an agreement. Taft admitted that the two men did not exactly see eye to eye on foreign policy, but that they did agree on a need to reduce the federal budget "as soon as practicable," as Eisenhower wrote in his memoirs. Privately, however, Taft insisted that Eisenhower agree to three specific demands: (1) Taft's people would be considered for positions in the new administration; (2) the new administration would initiate a tax reduction; and (3) that Tom Dewey would not be named secretary of state. Eisenhower probably knew what was coming. The press immediately dubbed the meeting, "the surrender at Morningside Heights."[9] Taft got what he wanted, and it was, in fact, an Eisenhower surrender. But Eisenhower also got what he wanted: a united party with Taft at his side, something that Dewey had failed to achieve just four years earlier. The attacks from the Democrats were brutal, but Eisenhower had to do it. He had to get the meeting out of the way, and move forward. The most important result was that Taft worked for the Eisenhower campaign. He hit twenty-one states in five weeks. And as the campaign neared its end, Taft, in a letter to the candidate, radiated optimism: "I feel confident you will be elected [,] probably by a very big majority."[10]

The ghosts of 1948 haunted the pollsters in 1952. Just four years earlier they had gotten it wrong, so they were more careful this time around. By late in the campaign, around August and September, the polls were pretty steady. In late August, the *St. Louis Post-Dispatch* was looking at the Electoral College and giving 238 electoral votes to Eisenhower (with another eighty-nine leaning in his direction) and 104 votes for Stevenson (with an additional fifty-four undecided but favoring Stevenson). Forty-eight electoral votes were identified as toss-ups. The toss-up states included Florida, Louisiana, Rhode Island, and Texas.[11] Within a few weeks, Gallup was giving Eisenhower a significant edge with over 50 percent of the popular votes, to Stevenson's 43 percent.[12] But the pollsters continued to look back at 1948. They made their predictions, but they also acknowledged that there was a large undecided vote that could, at the last minute, sway the election either way.[13]

Against all advice from his advisors, Eisenhower decided to campaign in the South, the first Republican in the twentieth century to do so. He seemed to see the shift in African American voter strength from the Republicans to the Democrats, leaving a large group of white Democrats stranded, with nowhere else to go. In 1948, they, of course, responded by forming the Dixiecrats. That political party had little impact on the 1948 election's final numbers, but it did show that white southerners were in the process of changing parties—from the Reconstruction-era Democrats to the Republicans. At the same time, Southern whites were essentially conservative. To Eisenhower (who seemed to keep all these ideas to himself) these points made for easy political pickings in the South. Eisenhower was an astute politician. The white South was moving into the Republican Party, and he knew it.

Eisenhower made three campaign swings into the South, always against the advice of those around him. In Atlanta, he was greeted by Georgia's Democratic Governor Herman Talmadge. That was followed by a ticker-tape parade down Peachtree Street. He went on to Jacksonville, Miami, Tampa, Birmingham, and Little Rock.[14] At each stop he was, of course, greeted as the hero of Normandy, but he was also received as a political candidate, a Republican who did not necessarily support civil rights for African Americans.

Eisenhower had always talked about the commonalities between what he called, "the progressive Southern Democrats and the progressive Northern Republicans." At one point, before he entered the campaign, he had asked Lodge if "it was so impossible that [Lodge] and a Senator like [moderate Alabama Senator] Lister Hill could be in the same party?"[15]

While Eisenhower tried to pull his divided party together, Stevenson was doing all he could to move as far away from Truman as possible. He knew that the Eisenhower campaign would try to associate him with Truman, make him out to be Truman's hand-picked successor, Harry's candidate. In August, in a by-mail interview with the *Oregon Journal*, Stevenson referred to "the mess in Washington," a phrase often used by Eisenhower and the Republicans to draw attention to the various scandals inside the Truman administration. Truman responded almost immediately, claiming that he knew of no "mess" in Washington.[16] The statement by Stevenson, as insignificant as it might seem, probably was designed to separate his campaign from Truman. And Truman did not like it: "I have come to the conclusion that you are embarrassed by having the President of the United States in your corner in this campaign," the president wrote in one of his many personal letters to himself.[17] But there was little he could do. Stevenson would run his own campaign.

There is hardly anything more telling in a political campaign than image, and in the age just before television (or at least before extensive cable television coverage) a candidate's tell, more than anything, was his performance as a speaker. In 1948, Truman was persuaded to give up his "wooden" speaking style, as one of his advisors described it, and speak extemporaneously to the crowds. The result was Truman's famous whistle-stop campaign tours through the nation's heartland. From the back of his train, the *Ferdinand Magellan*, Truman introduced his family, made a point or two to the crowd, and then moved on. Many Americans, for the first time, saw and heard the president of the United States, a man who was one of them. And they responded with votes. In contrast, Tom Dewey, filled with overconfidence and arrogance, lectured Americans. He was the "little man on the wedding cake," as Alice Longworth Roosevelt described him. In the final analysis, he failed to connect. In 1952, it was Eisenhower who seemed to learn the most from Truman's methods. Eisenhower was articulate. He was, in fact, a fairly eloquent writer. His campaign speeches, however, often seemed down right goofy, with mangled syntax and weak grammar. But he talked to the people of the country, and made every effort to reduce his speech patterns to their level. He spoke plainly, and conveyed concrete ideas that the average American could grasp. He often used examples, told personal stories, and even used props to make his points. At the same time, as Brownell pointed out in later years, he "was an absolutely magnetic personality as far as crowds were concerned."[18] James Reston of *The New York Times* observed in the summer of 1952, just before the convention, that "General Eisenhower's most vivid characteristic is his transparent sincerity and honesty. . . . This quality gets across quickly . . . to larger audiences in political rallies and on the television screen."[19]

Eisenhower also understood the need to keep the press close. Truman saw the significance of the press in 1948; he spent time playing cards and drinking bourbon with the pressmen on his campaign train. Even though they thought he would lose the election, the members of the press stayed close to the president and his campaign. In 1952, Eisenhower even took time to play golf with members of the press, and they returned the favor with press reports that were more favorable than those that Stevenson received. Eisenhower surely understood (and made good use of the fact) that anyone in 1952 would like to play a round of golf with a genuine American hero, and probably the next President of the United States.

Eisenhower is often portrayed as a political novice, a military figure (not unlike most military figures) who was brilliant at the workings of battlefield warfare, but who knew little of Washington politics. By most accounts, however, that was not true. Eisenhower was never a battlefield commander. In fact, his primary role in the war in Europe was to build a coalition of the world's biggest egos, bring them together, and force them to cooperate against a formidable enemy. He was, in effect, a politician who worked magic in the world of international politics. Washington's political scene in the 1950s was probably simple for a man whose political savvy had served to change the course of the world. "I read a lot of nonsense . . . about Eisenhower not being a politician," Eisenhower's press secretary, James Hagerty, told an interviewer later in his life, "and I think it's a lot of gosh darn nonsense. He hated and despised . . . the smallness and pettiness of everyday politics. But as far as intuitively and instinctively knowing what to do and how to do it, I think this guy was a master."[20] In addition, Eisenhower (unlike most politicians) had almost nothing to prove as president of the United States. He did not need to take credit for events. His ego was mostly in check. And as a moderate Republican, he was able and willing to compromise, work both sides of the aisle. Hagerty saw Eisenhower as a true leader: "He was not, and did not like or did not understand clubhouse politics, or the cheap and petty maneuvering of politics. . . . Indeed he had little patience with it. But to me, in the pure . . . usage of the term 'politician,' he was a pretty good one, because he got things done."[21]

In contrast, Stevenson delivered wonderful, eloquent, witty speeches, written mostly by thirty-four-year-old Arthur Schlesinger, Jr., and a group of the nation's greatest writers and pundits, known as the Elk's Club Group. They included playwright Robert Sherwood, novelist Herman Wouk, Archibald MacLeish, and Roosevelt's own speechwriter, Sam Rosenman. In the game of who was the best speaker, Stevenson certainly was the winner by a mile. In fact, some of the nation's leading figures gushed over Stevenson's style, wit, and antidotes. W. Gibson Harris wrote to William McCormick Blair (both prominent attorneys), "like no words I have ever heard from a politician." Harvard historian Milton Anastos wrote to Schlesinger, "We feel that Stevenson's speeches are in the very best literary tradition." A prominent economist in the Truman administration, William Batt, told Schlesinger that Stevenson's campaign was "the most literate campaign in our lifetime, perhaps in all our history."[22] But Stevenson sounded pompous to the average American, often reading from his witty scripts, and approaching the podium with his speeches in a leather-bound folio, "like an economics professor on his way to lecture," Alistair Cooke wrote.[23] He also surrounded himself with intellectuals, much like Roosevelt had. But for Stevenson, the desire to be a member of the nation's intelligentsia backfired. The Alsop brothers (Stewart and Joseph), the very bedrock of fifties journalism, famously described Stevenson as an "egghead," and the pejorative tag stuck—made all the worse by the candidate's baldness.[24] To most Americans, the election was between the General and the Egghead.

Success in 1952, however, would not be gauged by eloquence in speaking, or clever witticisms. It was about connecting with the audience. In the 2012 presidential election, Republican candidate Mitt Romney tried to slough off President Barak Obama's appealing speaking style. The strategy failed. But in 1952, Eisenhower made audiences realize that Stevenson's speaking style did not count. And for him the strategy worked. In response to criticisms that his speeches did not have the power and entertainment quality of Stevenson's, Eisenhower told a crowd in South Bend, Indiana:

> I have found in this business of going around the country carrying a political message [that] it would be very, very fine if one could command new and amusing language, witticisms to bring you a chuckle. Frankly, I have no intention of trying to do so. The subjects of which we are speaking . . . are not those that seem to me to be amusing.[25]

Arthur Krock, in *The New York Times* commented further: Eisenhower hopes that "the American people can be brought to resent [Stevenson's humorous speeches] as a wisecracking approach to weighty affairs and the mark of an essentially frivolous man."[26]

* * *

Richard Nixon played a major role in the 1952 campaign. Eisenhower had chosen Nixon to be his running mate for a number of reasons, but certainly because Nixon, throughout his life, had developed the reputation for being an "attack dog." In the 1952 campaign, he filled that bill. While Eisenhower took the high road, Nixon did what he did best: he hung close to the low road and went on the attack. Nixon's attacks, however, came to an abrupt end in mid-September when a story broke in the press that he had at his disposal a slush fund of between $16,000 and $18,000. The story was first reported in the *New York Post* on Thursday, September 18. The next day, from his train in Maryville, California, Nixon addressed the charge by pointing his finger at the Communists: "I was warned," he told the crowd, "that if I continued to attack the Communists . . . that they would continue to smear me."[27] For Nixon, the problem was immediate. One of the primary talking points for the Republican campaign had been "that mess in Washington," a direct reference to the corruption that had been uncovered in the Truman administration. Both Eisenhower and Nixon had been hitting the point hard on the campaign trail, insisting that a vote for them was a vote for good government and honesty in government.[28] Such a misstep, legal or not, might have given Eisenhower just the excuse he needed to kick Nixon off the ticket. Eisenhower responded by doing nothing. Nixon sat on the bubble and waited.

Two days later, on September 20, *The New York Times* published a little ditty, a poem, that seemed to hit at the significance of the scandal. It was titled, "They're Fixin' Mr. Nixon."

"We have often heard the shout,
'We must turn the rascal out.
The rate they're leading us to ruin isn't slow.'
But cleaning up their own backyard,
May be just a wee bit hard,
When millionaires are slipping them the dough."[29]

The pro-Stevenson *New Republic* reported that Nixon had received the money "from wealthy Republicans that have a certain political axe which they want young Nixon to wield. No one knows," the article continued, "how much more California gold may be involved."[30]

When the story hit the Eisenhower campaign train, which was then roaring through Iowa and Nebraska, there was a great deal of discussion about dumping Nixon from the ticket. Eisenhower's campaign manager, Herbert Brownell, told Eisenhower that the episode was severe enough that it might actually cause his defeat.[31] Eisenhower was scheduled to speak in Kansas City on the corruption issue in the Truman administration, but he feared that he would be heckled by the audience. So, he opened his speech by praising Nixon.[32] With the pressure mounting, Nixon announced, on September 21, that he would make a statement to the nation on the slush fund. Most thought he would use the speech to resign from the campaign, and there is some evidence that he intended to do just that.[33] But he was approached by Republican National Chairman Arthur Summerfield, who apparently convinced Nixon to stay on the campaign. Late that Sunday evening, September 21, Nixon and Eisenhower spoke on the telephone. "You know," Eisenhower told Nixon, "this is an awful hard thing for me to decide." Nixon responded by telling Eisenhower that "in matters like this . . . you've either got to shit or get off the pot." Eisenhower then suggested that Nixon "go on a nationwide television program and tell them anything there is to tell—everything you can remember. Tell them about any money you ever took." They ended their conversation with "Keep your chin up," from Eisenhower. And a "good luck" from Nixon.[34] Nixon also received a telegram from Thomas Dewey. Dewey told Nixon that Eisenhower had spoken to "a lot of his old friends," as Dewey presented it. And they all "except one" had argued that Nixon should leave the ticket. But Dewey pushed Nixon to hang on "and go on television. . . . At the conclusion of the program ask the people to wire in their verdict to you."[35] The next day, Nixon returned to Los Angeles where he locked himself in a hotel room and began writing what would become the "Checkers Speech."

It was on that day that another story broke, this one pointing to Stevenson, who had maintained a similar fund of his own.[36] But Stevenson barely addressed it. In a statement released by his campaign, Stevenson said, "There has never been any secret about the fact that I have tried to reduce the financial sacrifice of a number of men whom I induced to leave private employment to work for the State of Illinois."[37] He then released the names of the contributors, and then made his tax records available from the previous ten years.[38] Perhaps anticipating the revelation that he too had a slush fund at this disposal, Stevenson told *The New York Times* just after the Nixon story broke that it "would be wrong" to condemn Nixon "without all the evidence."[39] Clearly, Nixon's situation was more important because the Eisenhower-Nixon campaign was so focused on the corruption in Washington, and their willingness to stop it. The next day, Tuesday, September 23, Nixon arrived at the El Capitan Theater in Hollywood to deliver his speech. *The New York Times* called it variously "a masterpiece" and a "soap opera."[40] Nixon began by explaining that the fund was both legal and ethical, that the $18,000 went to pay his campaign expenses, and that he did not profit in any way from the fund. "[N]ot one cent of the $18,000 or any other money of that type ever went to me for my personal use." He continued by explaining that he was just an average American, that he had very little money, that his wife "sitting over there" was not on his Senate office payroll, and that without funding from supporters he would need to charge taxpayers for his various expenses. As evidence, he produced an audit by the accountants Price Waterhouse, and then he read a legal opinion by the Los Angeles law firm of Gibson, Dunn, and Crutcher that exonerated him of any wrongdoing. He followed that with his personal financial history, which was modest—even for the early 1950s. Then he added "One other thing I probably should tell you" that he had accepted a gift from a supporter, "A man down in Texas" who had sent his family a dog. His daughters had named it "Checkers. . . . And[sic] I just want to say right now," he added, "that regardless of what they say about it, we're gonna keep it." The remainder of the speech was mostly a political statement. He added that Stevenson had a similar fund, "in which a group of business people paid and helped to supplement the salaries of

State employees."[41] By some accounts, Eisenhower saw Nixon's speech as decisive and agreed immediately to keep him on the ticket.[42] But most likely, Eisenhower balked at making a quick decision. He sent a telegram to Nixon that began: "Your presentation was magnificent." But he made it clear that he had not yet made up his mind. He concluded the telegram with a genuine complement: "I cannot close this telegram," he wrote, "without saying that whatever personal admiration and affection I have for you—and they are very great—are undiminished."[43] Although that was certainly a positive response, it was not a confirmation that Nixon would remain on the ticket. Herbert Parmet has written that Eisenhower was not at all impressed by the speech, that he rammed a pencil through a piece of paper just as Nixon finished. He was particularly annoyed that the entire incident would force him to make public his own financial dealings.[44]

Eisenhower's reticence pushed Nixon to write his own resignation. His secretary, however, destroyed the letter.[45] Nixon wrote to Eisenhower demanding a decision, insisting that he would not agree to meet with the Eisenhower until he made a public statement keeping him on the ticket. Eisenhower again refused, but Nixon was privately assured that Eisenhower would finally agree to keep him on the ticket. Nixon made the trip to Eisenhower's train, then in Wheeling, West Virginia. On Wednesday, September 24, at 10 p.m., Nixon's plane landed in Wheeling. Eisenhower met him at the airport, put his arm around Nixon and said, "You're my boy." Nixon responded, "This is probably the greatest moment of my life."[46]

At the end of his speech, Nixon had intended to ask the American people to support him by sending their statements of approval to the Republican National Committee. But he was cut off before he could make the appeal. Nevertheless, the RNC received nearly 2 million calls and telegrams by the next morning, mostly in support of Nixon and his place on the Republican ticket.[47]

Nixon's speech also seemed to revitalize the Republican campaign. "The Republican drive," *The New York Times* reported, which "had been suffering from dissension, lassitude and pessimism, suddenly took fire." The next day, money began rolling into Nixon's Southern California campaign headquarters; his advisors there began calling the money "Dollars for Dick."[48] The speech also raised Nixon's recognition numbers. A Field Poll asked the question "Do you happen to remember the name of the Republican candidate for Vice President?" Before the "Checkers" speech, 83 percent could name Nixon. After the speech, that number jumped ten points.[49] By most accounts, Nixon's speech helped his campaign overall. James Reston at *The New York Times* wrote that the entire event "boomeranged" for the Democrats. "[O]ne of the most dramatic boomerangs, in fact, since Andrew Jackson turned the opposition attacks against his wife Rachel to great political advantage."

He continued that the secret Stevenson fund had made it difficult for Stevenson to argue that he was a symbol of change. Reston also pointed out that the incident unified the two wings of the Republican Party, and it served to move Nixon to center stage, making him a national figure really for the first time.[50] The Democrats also realized it. In a letter to Arthur Schlesinger, Jr., Wisconsin Congressman, Thomas Amlie, wrote "[S]o with a little corny histrionics, Sen. Nixon has been transformed from a shyster politician into a great Republican hero."[51]

One result of the event was the release of financial records and tax records of all the candidates. Stevenson and Sparkman released their tax information immediately, and Eisenhower announced that he would do the same "later on."[52] Nixon's people announced that their candidate would have nothing else to say about his finances, and financial corruption stopped being an issue in the campaign.

* * *

In early October, Eisenhower was on a campaign swing through the upper Midwest. He had been pushed by several of his advisors and speechwriters to take the opportunity to praise George Marshall. Eisenhower had been a Marshall protégé in World War II, and the two men had grown to be great admirers of each other. Marshall had, however, become a target of Joe McCarthy. McCarthy had found reason to blame Marshall for the collapse of Chiang Kai-shek's troops in China in 1949, and thus for the Communist takeover that year. McCarthy had even gone so far as to write a book, *America's Retreat from Victory: The Story of George Catlin Marshall*, accusing Marshall of being both unpatriotic and a Communist sympathizer who gave away China to the Communists.[53]

One of McCarthy's most ardent supporters was Indiana Senator William Jenner, a man intently disliked by Eisenhower. In early September, Eisenhower was scheduled to speak at the Field House at Butler University in Indianapolis. He was introduced by Jenner. Eisenhower's speech was designed to please the Midwestern Taftites adding a request that voters in Indiana vote a straight Republican ticket. But he did not mention Jenner. Following the speech, Jenner jumped to his feet and embraced Eisenhower. Eisenhower pulled away as flashbulbs went off. He later told Emmet Hughes that he "felt dirty from the touch of the man."[54]

Later in the month, in Peoria, Illinois, Eisenhower was contemplating several speeches that he would make in Wisconsin—Senator McCarthy's turf. He planned to pay tribute to his friend Marshall, praising him for his "profoundest patriotism to the service of America," a phrase he intended to use, a phrase that historians have called "mild praise."[55] In Wisconsin, any reference to Marshall would be perceived as a slash at McCarthy. By one account, McCarthy went to Eisenhower's hotel room in Peoria and asked that the praise for Marshall be removed from Eisenhower's speeches in Wisconsin. By other accounts, it was Wisconsin Governor Walter Kohler who asked Eisenhower to delete the part of the speech praising Marshall, insisting it was unnecessary.[56] In Green Bay, Eisenhower told the crowd that he would fight communism, using all constitutional means available. In Appleton, McCarthy's hometown, McCarthy introduced Eisenhower and stood by him for the entire speech. Eisenhower made no reference to McCarthy. On October 1, the train moved on to Milwaukee. On the trip of some three hours, McCarthy's men insisted again that Eisenhower cut the Marshall reference. Finally, after considerable pressure, Eisenhower gave in. "Take it out," he snarled.[57] Before some 8,500 people on October 3, Eisenhower pulled out his best anti-Communist chops. He spoke of the "treason" of communism inside "every department, every agency, every bureau, every section of our government." Washington, he said, was under the control of "men whose very brains were confused by the opiate of this deceit."[58] Most of this would have been of little significance, except that reporters in Milwaukee had received an advance copy of the speech that had included the Marshall reference, now omitted. Arthur Sulzberger, publisher of *The New York Times*, wrote to Sherman Adams, an Eisenhower advisor on the train with the candidate, "I am sick at heart."[59] And *The New York Times* reported that McCarthy had successfully pushed Eisenhower to remove the Marshall reference. However, McCarthy, Adams, and Eisenhower denied that McCarthy had sought, and then received, the omission.[60]

Stevenson, of course, tried to take advantage of the incident. In Milwaukee, five days later, he accused Eisenhower of giving in to McCarthy's demands, of compromising his own beliefs for the votes of the people of Wisconsin. Eisenhower had delivered his often-made comments directed at Stevenson's sense of humor, for cracking jokes during a serious campaign about serious issues. Stevenson, in Milwaukee, said: "My opponent has been worrying about my funny bone. I'm worried about his backbone."[61] By most accounts, Eisenhower had abandoned his friend, his mentor, for McCarthy's support.

McCarthy never really supported Eisenhower, but he did campaign for other Republicans throughout the country, especially those who carried the mantle of anticommunism. He spoke on behalf of Barry Goldwater in Arizona, for Frank Barrett in Wyoming, Zales Ecton in Montana, and Harry Cain in Washington. In Nevada, he threw his support to Senator George "Molly" Malone. In Indiana, he hailed Jenner as "a great American." He even went to Connecticut, where he spoke out against William Benton, a man, he said, who was worth "a hundred million dollars to the Kremlin." But he stayed clear of the Massachusetts race between the Republican Henry Cabot Lodge and the young John F. Kennedy, mostly at the behest of Joseph

Kennedy, whose sizable contribution to McCarthy's own campaign kept McCarthy out of Massachussetts.[62]

The first parts of the campaign revealed two completely different politicians. Eisenhower turned out to be the gregarious figure, the candidate who would come out to greet the people, often in a bathrobe. He was the candidate who could connect with voters—and with the press. He even played golf with them, and that relationship gave him a huge advantage over Stevenson. Here, in 1952, it was Eisenhower who the American people wanted to see. He was the hero of World War II, the man who had beaten the Nazis. Just four years earlier, it was Harry Truman, the President of the United States, who Americans wanted to see—and then to vote for. Stevenson's campaign is often described as dull. Rarely did Stevenson go out to meet the people. His crowds were smaller than Eisenhower's. He was not a glad-hander or baby-kisser. His campaign is still remembered for its oratory, its cleverness, its humor. And Stevenson never seemed to learn how to court the press or make much use of the new medium of television.

The whistle-stop tour, still a prominent part of the 1952 campaign, was about to be overshadowed by television. By 1956, and certainly by 1960, the whistle-stop campaign was a thing of the past, replaced by television, airplanes, and even by Hubert Humphrey's infamous bus in the 1960 West Virginia primary campaign. If the whistle-stop campaign was designed to show the American voter what the candidate and his family looked like (and sounded like). Then in 1952 more Americans were interested in seeing the General than seeing the Egghead.

* * *

On September 20, *The New York Times* speculated that 153 electoral votes would go to Eisenhower in the general election (with 142 additional votes listed as "Doubtful with an Edge to Eisenhower"). And 121 votes "probably for Stevenson," with an additional "Doubtful with an Edge to Stevenson" at forty-nine votes. Sixty-six votes were listed as "A toss-Up as of Now." The total was 531. That meant that 266 votes were needed to win. The toss-up states included Colorado (with six votes), Florida (with ten votes), Louisiana (with ten votes), Rhode Island (with four votes), Texas (with twenty-four votes), and Wisconsin (with twelve votes).[63] That, of course, meant that if Stevenson took the 121 votes "probably for Stevenson," and the forty-nine votes listed as "doubtful with an edge to Stevenson," he would still lose. He would, in fact, have to win most of the toss-up states to carry the election. On the other hand, Eisenhower could win easily (with twenty-nine votes to spare) if he combined his 153 votes with the 142 determined as "Doubtful with and Edge to Eisenhower." For Stevenson, the only good thing about the polls in 1952 was that they had been so wrong just four years earlier. For Eisenhower, the failures of the 1948 polls kept him in the fight, not at all willing to back off simply because the polls showed that he was on his way to a landslide victory. And of course, Truman, the surprise winner in 1948, was out on the stump in 1952, engaging voters—whether Stevenson wanted him there or not.

Eisenhower tried to place the blame for the conduct of the Korean War directly on Truman, and then by association on to Stevenson. Eisenhower found little wrong with Truman's decision to enter the war in June 1950. It was, after all, a direct response to Communist aggression. Instead, Eisenhower hit hard at the preinvasion situation that, he said, had left America's defenses in Asia open to attack from North Korea. Thus, he added, the war could have been avoided. In January 1950, Truman's secretary of state, Dean Acheson, had spoken at the National Press Club in Washington DC defining America's interests in Asia. In that speech, Acheson did not mention South Korea, or America's interests there. By some accounts, that omission (along with the rapid withdraw of American troops from the Korean peninsula) made it clear to the North Koreans (and to Moscow) that the United States would not defend South Korea against an attack.[64] On the campaign trail, Eisenhower often echoed that argument.

In Louisville, Stevenson responded immediately to Eisenhower's criticisms. He quoted Eisenhower, who, just after World War II, had said that the Americans and the Russians could live together—an apostasy in the early 1950s. Stevenson went on to claim that he had warned against a growing Russian menace as early as 1946. And that it was Eisenhower who had recommended withdrawing troops from the Korea peninsula. Stevenson added that nothing could have saved China from a Communist victory in 1949, and that Acheson, in his speech, had cut South Korea from the U.S. defensive perimeter in Asia on direct advice from General MacArthur.[65] In order to keep his cords cut with the Truman administration and its management of the war, Stevenson agreed with Eisenhower and other Republicans that the United States had removed its military from the Korean peninsula too quickly, and that it was a mistake to cross the 38th Parallel and invade north into North Korea in the fall of 1950.[66]

Stevenson's response in Louisville made it clear that Eisenhower had a significant hand in the conduct of the war—at least early on. In Champaign, Illinois, on October 2, Eisenhower changed his tack from responsibility (who was responsible for the war and for the execution of the war) to extraction (how should the United States get out of the war). It was here, for the first time, that Eisenhower used the phrase "Koreanization of the war." The United States, he said, should supply the South Korean forces with all they needed to fight the North. "Let the Asians fight the Asians," he said.[67] This was a pretty weak plan since the Chinese had already entered the war, and by 1952 they were more than capable of crushing the South Korean army. But it was a plan. And Stevenson had no plan.

Then, with no real warning, Eisenhower delivered a genuine October surprise. At a Masonic Temple in Detroit, he said he would go to Korea. Few recall that he expressed dismay about a solution to the problems facing the American military in Korea. And that he would go to Korea only to see the problems up close and determine for himself a solution to America's involvement.[68] Most Americans only heard that Eisenhower would take matters into his own steady hands and solve America's biggest problem. Almost immediately, a group of reporters turned to Sherman Adams, and said "That does it—Ike is in."[69]

Stevenson barely responded. Some have said that he could not respond, and that Eisenhower was well aware of that. But there was little Eisenhower could do in Korea. He was not a military figure in 1952. And the only thing he really did in Korea (after the election) was to boost the morale of American soldiers there. Stevenson might have made those points. But he was almost immediately distracted by an Illinois prison riot.

On October 31, just days before Election Day, there was a prison riot at Menard State Prison in Chester, Illinois. Stevenson was, of course, still governor of Illinois, and he felt a personal need to coordinate a plan against the riot. On October 31, Illinois State Troopers stormed the prison and relived the siege. As governor, it was important for Stevenson to be there, but it took away valuable campaign time at probably the most crucial moment in the campaign.[70]

* * *

The South and its relations with race has always been a challenging issue in American politics. That was particularly so in the first decade following World War II. The age-old issue of race was becoming volatile, and television had begun to show Americans that segregation in the South was, clearly, not a natural system. The election of 1948 had shown that the Democratic Party could not hold on to both white and black southerners, while at the same time white southerners (natural conservatives) were slowly trickling into the Republican Party, while Southern blacks were being given the vote in some areas in the South and moving slowly away from the party of Lincoln and into the Democratic Party.

Stevenson carried around some baggage that made the white South very uneasy. As governor of Illinois, he had supported a statewide FEPC that kept employers who received state funds from discriminating in hiring practices. He also supported a strong statewide civil rights program.[71] In an effort to keep the South in line, Stevenson agreed to accept Alabama Senator John

Sparkman on his ticket. But that gesture did little to bring along Southern politicos. Richard Russell, the powerful Georgia Senator, endorsed Stevenson, but he refused to campaign for him, and then went on a vacation trip to South America in the midst of Stevenson's campaign.[72] Harry Byrd of Virginia announced that he would not support Stevenson, although he never agreed to endorse Eisenhower.[73] South Carolina Governor Jimmy Byrnes, one of the true symbols of Southern segregation, actually worked for Eisenhower, campaigning in parts of Florida and making several television appearances on Eisenhower's behalf.[74] Southerners did not bolt the party in 1952, as they had four years earlier, but they might as well have.

On the other side of the fence, African Americans (both North and South) were leery of Stevenson's choice of Sparkman as a running mate. Sparkman was hardly a Southern segregationist, and he had opposed the Dixiecrat revolt in 1948. But it was not difficult for Republicans to win black votes by claiming that Sparkman was a Southern racist. If there was a civil rights leader in the early 1950s, it was Adam Clayton Powell, the Democratic representative in Congress from Harlem. Powell confronted Stevenson, insisting that he take a more forthright stand on civil rights, or he threatened, African Americans would boycott the election.[75] Stevenson was never able to straddle the fence on race; he was never able to keep both Southern whites and African Americans satisfied.

The Tidelands issue was not about race, but it was about states' rights. And states' rights was about race relations in the South. The Tidelands had turned Southern governors (particularly in Louisiana and Texas) against Truman. Truman had agreed with the 1947 Supreme Court ruling that gave the Tideland reserves (and the revenue stream in oil and natural gas that came with it) to the federal government and not the states. And, by most accounts, Stevenson followed Truman's lead.[76] The issue was, of course, about federal encroachment on Southern states' rights, and the South (not just the Gulf South) hated it. Nixon, probably more than anyone, used the Tidelands issue to divide the Democrats, claiming in August, that "a vote for Stevenson will be a vote for the . . . insatiable Truman program of building up Federal power by tearing down States' rights."[77] Just before the election, Eisenhower said that, if elected, he would push Congress to relinquish the Tidelands to the states. It was a smart tactic; it kept him from campaigning against the Supreme Court. He then, in mid-October, headed off to Texas and Louisiana on his third trip into the South.[78] In late August, Texas Governor Allan Shivers had made a pilgrimage to Springfield to visit with Stevenson, and by most accounts Shivers agreed to throw his support to Stevenson if he would soften his stance on the Tidelands issue, and thus on states' rights. But Shivers came away from the meeting disappointed and immediately announced that he would not vote for the Stevenson-Sparkman ticket.[79] Shivers then organized a large Democrats-for-Eisenhower movement in Texas that caused a split in that state's politics for the next decade. Shivers's tilt toward Eisenhower was opposed by House Speaker Sam Rayburn from Texas and Texas Senator Lyndon Johnson. Both Rayburn and Johnson gave a half-hearted effort toward Stevenson's 1952 campaign in Texas.[80] It was, however, the Tidelands issue (along with the efforts of Shivers) that pushed Texas into the Republican column in 1952.

* * *

Stevenson changed the very face of American politics when he swung the door open on campaign advertising in 1952 with an unassuming prime-time half-hour televised speech. The speech preempted *I Love Lucy*, at the time the number-one rated television program in the country. His campaign headquarters received a good deal of hate mail for their effort, and it became clear that the old school, long, drawn out political campaign speech did not hold the interest of American voters. The Democrats had hired Joseph Katz, a renowned Baltimore ad man. Katz purchased eighteen, half-hour time spots for television. He made a point of purchasing the time at the beginning of the campaign, which kept the price down, but more importantly it reflected a need to get Stevenson's face before the American voter as soon as possible. Stevenson was, of course, the lesser known of the two candidates—by far.[81]

Eisenhower and his people responded quickly. They retained at least three ad agencies, the most important being Ted Bates and Company and their heavy hitter, Rosser Reeves. Reeves used (what would be called today) focus groups to conclude that political speeches (like those given by Stevenson) were too long, too boring, and much too confusing to hold the attention of American audiences for any length of time.

Reeves initiated an advertising package for the Eisenhower campaign that included the "spot." In a memo, Reeves explained that "a spot is a 15-second or 1-minute announcement on radio—or a 20 second or 1-minute announcement on television." This "RADIO OR TV 'SPOT' CAN DELIVER MORE LISTENING FOR LESS MONEY THAN ANY OTHER FORM OF ADVERTISING." Reeves produced several of these "spots," and most were effective. One, scheduled to air in mid-October, explored the frustrations that many Americans were having in 1952: "WOMAN: 'My husband makes more money today . . . but we can't buy nearly as much food.'" "EISENHOWER: The Administration's own figures show that today people can afford less butter, less fruit, less milk. Yes, it's time for a change." "ANNOUNCER: 'a paid film.'"[82] In the last two weeks of the campaign, the Ted Bates Company made available to local and state campaign committees twenty-five TV and radio "spots" that were short and to the point: "General," an all-American couple states, "the administration tells us we never had it so good." "Eisenhower: Can that be true when America is billions in debt . . . when prices have doubled, when taxes break our backs . . . and when we are still fighting in Korea? It's tragic . . . it's time for a change!"[83] Stevenson responded with another made-for-TV documentary. This half-hour-to-hour-long event was much less effective than Eisenhower's spot ads, but really no less ground breaking. Stevenson did not understand television, and he seldom watched. But his campaign staff convinced him that he needed to be seen in order to win the election. The Stevenson documentary, probably the first of its kind, showed the candidate conducting his daily routine—in an attempt to show his personality, that he was a normal person and not an "egghead" or a "sidesaddle Adlai." He was shown working, relaxing, even shaving and blowing kisses.[84] But viewers had to tune in to Stevenson's documentary. Eisenhower's "spots" were much more effective. They hit viewers like modern commercials; viewers saw them whether they wanted to or not.

The 1950s was also a time of "television visiting," when family and friends without televisions would often visit those who owned TVs. Perhaps as many as 53 percent of Americans watched the campaign and were exposed to its two advertising campaigns.[85] There had been some advertising before 1952, of course, but it was mostly focused on radio or in the print media. It was in the 1952 campaign that television first played an important role in national politics.

Those who study elections want to look at the cost of TV ads. And almost certainly, Republicans outspent the Democrats by a wide margin.[86] But it seems likely that newspapers continued to have a strong stranglehold on the electorate in 1952. That is, newspapers were more significant in the outcome of the election than television. Not until the 1960 campaign would television play a major role in a presidential election. And not really until the 1964 campaign between Johnson and Goldwater would television ads become a deciding factor in the outcome. In 1952, television seemed to open the way for the future when it did have a major impact on the Republican convention, when Taft's people decided to exclude television cameras from an important credentials committee meeting, angering some very influential Chicago journalists and operatives. The Chicago press (and the national press) pulled away from Taft's candidacy, and began to focus more squarely on Eisenhower, making him the underdog.

Eisenhower won over the national print press—probably overwhelmingly. That certainly had a great deal to do with his personal relationship with *New York Herald-Tribune* executive William Robinson, allowing Eisenhower to pull the *New York Herald-Tribune* to his side. And in those years, the *Herald-Tribune* was probably as important as *The New York Times*.[87] *Time*, *Life*, and *Newsweek* also supported Eisenhower, although not overtly.

* * *

When the dust settled, Eisenhower won easily. He took the popular vote by almost 11 percent. The Electoral College was much more decisive. There, Eisenhower won 442 votes to Stevenson's 89. Stevenson took only the South. By any analysis, Eisenhower's victory was a landslide.[88]

Perhaps the most important aspect of the 1952 presidential election is the simplest point: the Democratic domination of the government had come to an end; it was the end of the New Deal-Fair Deal era. The Great Depression was over. The war was over. Under new Republican leadership, America could now get back on the track to normalcy—or at least some semblance of normalcy.

Of course, the most important question was why? Why did Americans cast their vote in such overwhelming numbers for the Republican presidential candidate in 1952? There is no doubt that personality played an important part in that. Eisenhower had everything it took to be President of the United States. It was a time of troubles in the world. The Soviet Union was flexing its muscles on the world stage. The Cold War was at its height. The Soviets had exploded an atomic bomb—long before anyone expected it. And most Americans believed that Western Europe was in Moscow's cross hairs. China had fallen to communism and was threatening Asia. Who better to take the reins of government than Eisenhower? He had dealt with the Russians on several levels. And if the Cold War turned hot he would be there as a military leader, a diplomat, the leader of the nation. Eisenhower-as-president had, in fact, invoked the common use of the word "apathy." Americans no longer needed to worry about world affairs. Let Ike handle it.

Eisenhower was also perceived as clean ("as a hound's tooth"), honest, upright, all those strong characteristics. Truman was never perceived as a crook, but his administration was seen as corrupt, and his party had been in office too long. Everything that was perceived as bad about the Democrats was projected onto Stevenson. Stevenson recognized that, of course, and tried desperately to separate himself from Truman, but it never really worked. Stevenson became Truman's successor by default, the successor to the Democratic Party legacy.

The Republicans had also built a new geographic coalition that would serve them well for at least two decades. Gone was the old liberal/moderate industrial Northeast. After 1952, the new Republican coalition would be anchored by Midwestern conservatives, and boosted by their allies in the conservative West. Increasingly, the conservative white South would become a part of that coalition. This new geographic Republican coalition was much more conservative, and much less willing to work with the Democrats.

Eisenhower also won big in just about all sections of the nation. He won in New York, California, Illinois, and Michigan. He was the strongest in the Far West, taking over 57 percent of the total there—almost 9 percentage points above Dewey's count in that region just four years before. Eisenhower, in fact, won every state west of the Mississippi.[89] It was in the South that Eisenhower achieved his biggest gains and his biggest surprise. It is important to keep in mind that in 1952 the South was still segregated and African Americans, generally, could not vote. By all accounts, Stevenson took the South, just as Democrats had taken the Solid South since Reconstruction. But clearly Eisenhower had made significant inroads—inroads that were a portent for the future. Stevenson won by good totals in Arkansas, Alabama, Georgia, and Mississippi. He also took Truman's Missouri, Kentucky, Louisiana, and the Carolinas—but by fairly small margins. Eisenhower's victories in the big electoral states of Texas and Virginia were particularly important. But he also took Florida and Tennessee.[90] Four years later, Stevenson would take back Missouri but he would lose Louisiana in a second losing cause.

Stevenson won the African American vote, the Italian vote, organized labor, and the Jewish vote. But Eisenhower won in the big categories of the day that counted. He won the female vote, really the first time that women had been counted and courted. By most accounts, American women opposed the Korean War and America's involvement in it. American mothers, like in most wars, feared that their sons and husbands would be taken from them to fight a war that they saw as inconsequential, even useless. When Eisenhower-the-candidate promised he would go to Korea, most Americans believed he would end the war, end the stalemate, and bring American boys home. Opposition to the war, apparently, sent American women to the polls in great numbers.[91]

If there is a headline to this election it is that Eisenhower won the white-collar vote, or the middle-class vote that had begun their move to the nation's suburbs. There is an historical truism that by 1900 Americans had moved from the country into the cities. But by 1952, they had moved from the cities (where they had voted overwhelmingly Democratic) into the suburbs where they voted for Eisenhower in 1952. This was a major realignment, and as Louis Harris wrote in 1954, "No political candidate can overlook them after 1952." One in three white-collar voters in the North who had voted Democratic before 1952, voted for Eisenhower in 1952.

Eisenhower also won independent voters, those who had shifted their votes between Democrats and Republicans over time. They went for Eisenhower by a margin of almost three-to-one.[92] Who were these people? Before the war, they were mostly Democrats, underprivileged, often first-generation immigrants, raised during the Depression, and they needed the support (or believed they needed the support) of the federal government. In fact, Franklin Roosevelt won over these voters—mostly for foreign policy reasons. After the war, this group threw their support to Dewey—a moderate internationalist. It was then that this group began its movement to the suburbs and into the Republican Party, easy pickings for Eisenhower. They moved for several reasons. The federal government neglected to provide enough housing in the cities for some of these people. There was also a great middle-class desire to own their personal homes just after the war. And moving to the suburbs meant moving from blue collar to white collar, from immigrant status to post-immigrant status. There was also a new respectability in the suburbs. And the suburbs were conservative. Politics there was often remote. Property owners always oppose higher taxes, and it was the Republicans in 1952 who promised to lower taxes. Those who supported Eisenhower also came to believe that the federal government had gone too far on regulation, particularly the regulation of big business. At the same time, Eisenhower was perceived as the new modern, and less strident than the Democrats. A vote for Eisenhower in 1952 meant a vote for the future. The Democrats represented the past, the party of corruption and war.

Eisenhower needed the support of these moderate suburbanites to offset the normally huge Democratic big-city vote. He needed a huge defection from the Democratic Party. And he got it.

Then, there was Eisenhower himself. Eighty-nine percent of those who voted for Eisenhower said they did so because of his personality. Only 70 percent of those voting for Stevenson saw his personality as a deciding factor in their vote.[93] These white-collar voters liked Ike. He was nonpartisan, middle of the road, clean as a hound's tooth, and an internationalist. Samuel Lubell called him "a clean sheet of paper."[94]

But was it a Republican victory? The answer is probably "no." Eisenhower ran ahead of his party, nationally. But the Republicans gained only small majorities in both the houses of Congress, giving them a slight nine-seat majority in the House and only a one-seat majority in the Senate.[95] John Kennedy beat Lodge in Massachusetts; Stewart Symington, a Democrat, won in Missouri; and Jenner and McCarthy both held on in Indiana and Wisconsin, but only by a squeak. Both Jenner and McCarthy retained their Senate seats, but both ran behind Eisenhower. In fact, it has often been assumed that had Taft won the Republican nomination (and run for president on the Republican ticket in 1952) that Jenner, McCarthy, and probably Barry Goldwater, would have lost their seats to Democrats in that election.[96]

So, was the 1952 election a rebuke of Republicanism? The Democrats thought so. Lyndon Johnson concluded that the election was "A personal triumph for Eisenhower and *not* a Republican victory." The Republicans only secured control of the House and the Senate by small majorities "behind a candidate who rolled up one of the most astounding votes in history."[97] There was a similar outlook in Stevenson's own files. "Eisenhower's victory was a personal one in every sense of the word. It in no way constituted a victory for the Republican party or the ideas associated with the Republican party. . . . It cannot be construed as a repudiation of the principles of the New

Deal and the Fair Deal."[98] And then George Reedy, a Democratic Party operative in this period, called the election a "rebuke" because the Republicans had won control of both houses by such a small amount.[99] In 1954, just two years later, the Republicans lost control of both houses of Congress. There was a popular saying at the time: "America likes Ike, but they don't like the Republicans."

There were other observations. Eisenhower won back the nation's farmers.[100] Farmers had voted Democratic during the Roosevelt-Truman years mostly because of farm supports and other New Deal-type programs. By 1952, farmers (always conservative) had begun to make a strong move back into the Republican Party. Farmers, outside the South, voted for Eisenhower by a whopping 79 percent.[101] Eisenhower also won the Polish vote, the Irish vote, Germans, and middle-aged voters. Stevenson was successful with the Jewish vote, the union vote, and the youth vote.

On election night, Jake Arvey, the notorious Democratic Party political boss from Chicago, said, "The suburbs beat us." Essentially, he was correct. Only Philadelphia and Detroit outlasted the Republican votes of their suburbs. Chicago, Cleveland, and even New York went to Eisenhower. Eisenhower carried seventeen of thirty-five cities with populations over 300,000. In 1948, Dewey had carried only three.[102]

The presidential campaign of 1952 did not realign the parties as some big elections did. But it did change both parties significantly. Gone was the New Deal-Fair Deal Democratic Party of Roosevelt and Truman. Democrats may have tried to keep that hope alive into the next decades, but with Eisenhower's election that era in American history came to an end. The 1952 campaign was also the beginnings of a major split in the Republican Party. This split had been around a while, some might argue since at least the presidential campaign of 1912. But with Eisenhower's moderation, it was only a matter of time when a GOP leader on the Republican Right would stand up and take the lead within the party against the Dewey-Eisenhower moderates. That, of course, would be Barry Goldwater. He would be swamped in 1964 by the Lyndon Johnson landslide, but that ignominious defeat would lead the Republicans to reassess and focus their party's image and reemerge as a majority party under Ronald Reagan in 1980. The 1952 presidential campaign, as seemingly insignificant as it was, was the beginning of that change.

It was a big victory for Eisenhower, moderation, and an end to the New Deal-Fair Deal era. The 1952 campaign can be analyzed and then analyzed again. But it can be most easily summed up by Edward R. Morrow: "Too many people liked Ike."[103]

Election Statistics
(Electoral College) 1952

Alabama	Stevenson	11		Nebraska	Eisenhower	6
Arizona	Eisenhower	4		Nevada	Eisenhower	2
Arkansas	Stevenson	8		New Hampshire	Eisenhower	4
California	Eisenhower	32		New Jersey	Eisenhower	15
Colorado	Eisenhower	6		New Mexico	Eisenhower	4
Connecticut	Eisenhower	8		New York	Eisenhower	48
Delaware	Eisenhower	3		North Carolina	Stevenson	14
Florida	Eisenhower	10		North Dakota	Eisenhower	4
Georgia	Stevenson	12		Ohio	Eisenhower	25
Idaho	Eisenhower	4		Oklahoma	Eisenhower	8
Illinois	Eisenhower	27		Oregon	Eisenhower	6
Indiana	Eisenhower	13		Pennsylvania	Eisenhower	22
Iowa	Eisenhower	10		Rhode Island	Eisenhower	4
Kansas	Eisenhower	8		South Carolina	Stevenson	8
Kentucky	Stevenson	10		South Dakota	Eisenhower	4
Louisiana	Stevenson	10		Tennessee	Eisenhower	11
Maine	Eisenhower	5		Texas	Eisenhower	24
Maryland	Eisenhower	9		Utah	Eisenhower	4
Massachusetts	Eisenhower	16		Vermont	Eisenhower	3
Michigan	Eisenhower	20		Virginia	Eisenhower	12
Minnesota	Eisenhower	11		Washington	Eisenhower	9
Mississippi	Stevenson	8		West Virginia	Stevenson	8
Missouri	Eisenhower	13		Wisconsin	Eisenhower	12
Montana	Eisenhower	4		Wyoming	Eisenhower	3

Notes

CHAPTER 1

1. James MacGregor Burns, "Is Our Two-Party System in Danger?" *The New York Times Magazine* (Sept. 7, 1952), 13.

2. Samuel Lubell, *Revolt of the Moderates* (New York, 1956), 2–3, 265.

3. Louis Harris, *Is There A Republican Majority? Political Trends, 1952–1956* (New York, 1954), 199. See also Angus Campbell, et. al., *The Voter Decides: A Study of the Voter's Perceptions, Attitudes, and Behaviors . . . Based on a Survey of the 1952 Election* (New York, 1954), 33–35.

4. *Ibid.*

5. Taft always insisted that "me-tooism" was the problem of the Republican Party, and that he would have nothing to do with "me-tooism." See *Life* (Jan. 28, 1952).

6. Dwight D. Eisenhower, *Mandate for Change: 1953–1956* (Garden City, NY, 1963), 4–5. The correspondent was Virgil Pinckney.

7. DDE to Arthur Eisenhower (Oct. 20, 1943), EP, Eisenhower Library, Abilene, Kansas. Arthur Eisenhower has always been considered more conservative than Dwight.

8. Stephen Ambrose, *Eisenhower* (New York, 1983), I, 269.

9. On the 1944 campaign, see David M. Jordan, *FDR, Dewey, and the Election of 1944* (Bloomington, IN, 2011), *passim*; Ronald Steel, *Walter Lippmann and the American Century* (Boston, MA, 1980), 412; Melvyn Dubovsky and Warren Van Tyne, *John L. Lewis: A Biography* (Urbana, IL, 1986), 327.

10. Harry S. Truman, *Memoirs* (Garden City, NY), I, 12.

11. *NYT* (Mar. 2, 1945).

12. Dwight D. Eisenhower, *Crusade in Europe* (Garden City, NY, 1948), 444. In 1958 Truman denied that he ever made this statement, but that was at a time when the Truman-Eisenhower relationship was at a low point. Omar Bradley recalled Truman's

statement. See Omar Bradley, *A Soldier's Story* (New York, 1951), 444. See also Steve Neal, *Harry and Ike: The Partnership that Remade the Postwar World* (New York, 2001), 44; and Harry C. Butcher, *My Three Years with Eisenhower: The Personal Diary of Captain Harry C. Butcher, USNR* (New York, 1946), 434. Years later, Eisenhower's Press Secretary, James Hagerty, told an interviewer that Eisenhower had told him that the incident had, in fact, occurred. See James Hagerty interview, COHC.

13. Quoted in John Gunther, *Eisenhower: The Man and the Symbol* (New York, 1952), 133. In one form or another, General William T. Sherman had said "I will not accept if nominated and will not serve if elected."

14. Joel Seidman, *American Labor from Defense to Reconversion* (Chicago, 1953), 240–41. In the last half of 1946, consumer prices increased by nearly 15 percent, and food prices increased by nearly 30 percent. Those increases are reflected in the real wage statistics cited here. See also R. Alton Lee, *Truman and Taft-Hartley: A Question of Mandate* (Lexington, KY, 1966), 17.

15. *NYT* (Nov. 12, 17, Dec. 1, and 13, 1945); *Life* (Nov. 22, and Dec. 9, 1945), 16. William E. Leuctenburg, *In the Shadow of FDR: From Harry Truman to Ronald Reagan* (Ithaca, NY, 1989), 23; *Newsweek* (Sept. 13, 1946). Alonzo Hamby has concluded that Truman chose to stay out of the campaign. See Hamby, *Beyond the New Deal: Harry S. Truman and American Liberalism* (New York, 1973), 136–37. On this same point, see Harold F. Gosnell, *Truman's Crises: A Political Biography of Harry S. Truman* (Westport, CT, 1980), 315.

17. *U.S. News* (Nov. 15, 1946).

18. *Newsweek* (Nov. 18, 1946).

19. William S. White, *The Taft Story* (New York, 1954), 57.

20. Gallup Poll cited in *Reader's Digest* (Dec. 1947); *Time* (Dec. 2, 1946).

21. *Ibid.*; *Life*, (Dec. 2, 1946).

22. Louis Galambos and Alfred D. Chandler, Jr., eds., *The Papers of Dwight D. Eisenhower*, (Baltimore, MD, 1983) #1700 (Aug. 21, 1947), 1890. Also in Eisenhower Diary (Aug. 21, 1947), EP, Eisenhower Library.

23. Gunther, *Eisenhower*, 133.

24. Eisenhower Diary (Sept. 18, 1947), EP, Eisenhower Library.

25. *Ibid.*, (Oct. 31, 1947).

26. *Ibid.*, (Oct. 16, 1947).

27. *Ibid.*, (Jan. 12, 1948); see also Galambos and Chandler, eds., notes in *Papers of Eisenhower*, 2192–94.

28. *NYT* (Jan. 13, 1949). For the difficulty Eisenhower had in composing the letter, see James Forrestal, *Forrestal Diaries* (New York, 1951), 365–66; and note to Lynn Townsend White in, Galambos and Chandler, eds., *Papers of Eisenhower* #2016 (Jan. 29, 1948), 2211. See also Peter Lyon, *Eisenhower: Portrait of a Hero* (Boston, MA, 1974), 379–80; and William B. Pickett, *Eisenhower Decides to Run: Presidential Politics and Cold War Strategy* (Chicago, 2000), 39–40.

29. The Finder Letter is available in several places. The most accessible may be Galambos and Chandler, eds., *Papers of Eisenhower* #1998 (Jan. 22, 1948), 2191–93. A copy is also in *NYT* (Jan. 24, 1948). See also Kevin McCann, *Man From Abilene: Dwight Eisenhower, A Story of Leadership* (New York, 1952), 146–47.

30. Quoted in Gunther, *Eisenhower,* 137. Eisenhower told Bedell Smith, "I have experienced a great sense of personal freedom that I was rapidly losing." Eisenhower Diary (Jan. 28, 1948), EP, Eisenhower Library.

31. Polls that made this observation were fairly common. See Gallup Poll in *Newsweek* (Oct. 6, 1947); *Public Opinion Quarterly* (Summer, 1948); Roper Poll in *Fortune* (June, 1948).

32. Reinhold Niebuhr to James Loeb (June 23, 1948), ADA Papers, ADA Administrative Files, WSHS, Madison.

33. "Statement on Political Policy" (April 11, 1948), in *ibid.*

34. Eisenhower Diary (April 12, 1948), EP, Eisenhower Library.

35. *Time* (April 19, 1948).

36. *NYT* (July 4–5, 1948).

37. Eisenhower Diary (July 5, 1948), EP, Eisenhower Library.

38. *Newsweek* (July 7, 1948).

39. Galambos and Chandler, eds., *Papers of Eisenhower* (July 8, 1948), 129; *NYT* (July 3, and 6, 1948). See also *Time* (July 12, 1948).

40. For a more in depth analysis from this viewpoint, see Gary Donaldson, *Truman Defeats Dewey* (Lexington, KY, 1999), 204–20.

41. Samuel Lubell, *The Future of American Politics* (New York, 1964), 241.

42. *Ibid.*, 241.

43. Burns, "Is our Two-Party System in Danger?" 13.

CHAPTER 2

1. Stevenson's largest margin of victory came from Cook County, Illinois. Douglas won easily as well, but by a narrower margin. See Jeff Broadwater, *Adlai Stevenson: The Odyssey of a Cold War Liberal* (New York, 1994), 83; Porter McKeever, *Adlai Stevenson: His Life and Legacy* (New York, 1989), 126–27.

2. Humphrey had been the mayor of Minneapolis and won a Minnesota Senate seat that year. Johnson defeated Coke Stevenson for a Texas Senate seat by a suspect 87 votes. Kennedy won his House seat in 1946. He defeated Henry Cabot Lodge for a Massachusetts Senate seat in 1952.

3. After defeating Chicago Alderman Paul Douglas in the Democratic primary, McKeough lost to Brooks in the November general election.

4. John Bartlow Martin, *Adlai Stevenson of Illinois* (Garden City, NY, 1976), 222. See also George W. Ball, *The Past Has Another Pattern: Memoirs* (New York, 1982), 152.

5. McKeever, *Adlai Stevenson*, 94–101, 140–412.

6. Martin, *Adlai Stevenson of Illinois,* 223.

7. McKeever, *Adlai Stevenson*, 94–106.

8. Walter Johnson, ed., *The Papers of Adlai E. Stevenson: Washington to Springfield, 1941–1948* (Boston, MA, 1973), 393. The letter was to Edward G. Miller, Truman's Assistant Secretary of State. See also Martin, *Adlai Stevenson of Illinois,* 266–67; and Broadwater, *Adlai Stevenson,* 72. Even Richard Daly lost in 1946—for

the only time in his political career, running for sheriff of Cook County. Kennelly turned out to be one of Chicago's worst mayors.

9. John Bartlow Martin wrote: "Despite his powerful appeal to intellectuals, he was not really himself an intellectual." Martin, *Adlai Stevenson of Illinois*, 473.

10. Ball, *The Past Has Another Pattern*, 169.

11. John Kenneth Galbraith, *A Life in Our Times* (New York, 1982), 289.

12. In fact, Stevenson may have been right. With some success, Republicans, through the 1950s, attacked as radicals all Democrats running for public office who had joined the ADA. Stevenson also refused to join the American Civil Liberties Union (ACLU) for many of the same reasons.

13. Quoted in Steven M. Gillon, *Politics and Vision: The ADA and American Liberalism, 1947–1985* (New York, 1987), 48.

14. Walter Johnson, ed., *The Papers of Adlai Stevenson: Governor of Illinois, 1949–1953* (Boston, MA, 1973), 225. See also *Life* (Mar. 24, 1952). Here, *Life* says of Stevenson: "Sometimes he even sounds like a Republican."

15. Quoted in Martin, *Adlai Stevenson of Illinois*, 511.

16. *Ibid.*, 436.

17. *Ibid.*, 405–07. The full text of Stevenson's deposition in the Hiss case is in *NYT* (Oct. 15, 1952). The deposition was taken on June 2, 1949. See also Allen Weinstein, *Perjury: The Hiss-Chambers Case* (New York, 1978), 508–12.

18. Weinstein, *Perjury*, 450; *NYT* (Oct. 15, 1952).

19. Quoted in Weinstein, *Perjury*, 481; Martin, *Adlai Stevenson of Illinois*, 450.

20. Weinstein, *Perjury*, 469.

21. See statements and speeches in Johnson, ed., *Papers of Adlai Stevenson: Washington to Springfield*, 369–82. See also Martin, *Adlai Stevenson of Illinois*, 255–56.

22. See speeches reflecting this in Johnson, ed., *Papers of Adlai Stevenson: Governor of Illinois*, 135–46, 167, and 296–314. Stevenson's attitude toward the Soviets during the early days of the U.N. can be found in reflections by Henry Wallace. See John Morton Blum, ed., *The Price of Vision: The Diary of Henry A. Wallace, 1942–1946* (New York, 1973), 439–40.

23. Martin, *Adlai Stevenson of Illinois*, 418.

24. *Ibid.*, 486–88.

25. *Ibid.*, 488.

26. *Ibid.*, 487–88.

CHAPTER 3

1. Eisenhower Diary (Oct. 28, 1950), EP, Eisenhower Library.

2. Eisenhower, *Mandate for Change*, 13–14.

3. *Ibid.*, 14; Herbert S. Parmet, *Eisenhower and the American Crusade* (New York, 1972), 35–36.

4. Eisenhower Diary (Nov. 25, 1949), EP, Eisenhower Library.

5. On Eisenhower's internationalism, see Robert Griffith, "Dwight D. Eisenhower and the Corporate Commonwealth," *American Historical Review* (Feb. 1982), 116–17;

and Robert Griffith, *Ike's Letters to a Friend* (Lawrence, KN, 1984), 116. See also Herbert Brownell, *Advising Ike: The Memoirs of the Attorney General* (Lawrence, KN, 1993), 92.

6. Eisenhower Diary (Nov. 6, 1950), EP, Eisenhower Library. William Robinson also believed this. See William Robinson Papers, 1932–1969, Box 2, in *ibid.*

7. Ernest T. Weir and Harold Talbot to Eisenhower, Eisenhower Diary (Oct. 29, 1951), in *ibid.*

8. Eisenhower Diary, (July 10, 1951), in *ibid.*

9. Quoted in *Time* (Sept. 24, 1951). Herbert Brownell (an early Eisenhower supporter) often complained of this problem. See Brownell interview, ELOHC. And Brownell, *Advising Ike*, 92–93.

10. Eisenhower to Duff (Oct. 14, 1951) in Edwin N. Clark, "Curriculum Vita: Eisenhower for President: Preconvention Activities," unpublished manuscript (n.d.) 43–45, in Edwin N. Clark Papers, Eisenhower Library.

11. *Time* (Sept. 24, 1951). For a good analysis of the origins of the Dewey-Duff controversy, see Richard Norton Smith, *Thomas E. Dewey and His Times* (New York, 1982), 495–99.

12. *Saturday Evening Post* (May 31, 1952); Henry Cabot Lodge, *The Storm Has Many Eyes: A Personal Narrative* (New York, 1973), 88–91. In September, 1951, Lodge flew to Paris to try and convince Eisenhower to run. See Eisenhower, *Mandate for Change,* 16–18; Smith, *Dewey*, 578–79; William J. Miller, *Henry Cabot Lodge: A Biography by William Miller* (New York, 1967), 236.

13. Sherman Adams (then governor of New Hampshire) to Lodge, in *NYT* (Jan. 7, 1952). The quoted letter was written December 17, 1951. See also Lodge, *The Storm Has Many Eyes*, 95–96; and Sherman Adams, *First-Hand Report: The Inside Story of the Eisenhower Administration* (London, 1962), 25.

14. *NYT* (Jan. 8, 1952); New York *Herald-Tribune* (Jan. 8, 1952). A text of this speech can also be found in William Robinson Papers, 1932–1969, Eisenhower Library.

15. Eisenhower to Clay (Oct. 3, 1951), EP, Eisenhower Diary, Eisenhower Library.

16. Adams to Lodge (Dec. 12, 1951), Robertson Papers, 1932–1969, transcript of telephone conversation, Eisenhower Library.

17. Lodge to Adams (Jan. 4, 1952), Henry Cabot Lodge, Jr., Papers, Lodge-Eisenhower Correspondence, MHS, Boston. See also Lodge to Adams (Jan. 4, 1952), EP, Papers as President, 1953–1961 (Ann Whitman Files) Admin. Series, Eisenhower Library.

18. Eisenhower to Lodge (Mar. 18, 1952), Lodge Papers, Lodge-Eisenhower Correspondence, MHS.

19. Eisenhower, *Mandate for Change,* 18.

20. Eisenhower Diary (Jan. 10, 1952), EP, Eisenhower Library. See also Robert H. Ferrell, ed., *The Eisenhower Diaries* (New York, 1981), 209.

21. A good source on Cochran and her wartime exploits is Molly Merryman, *Clipped Wings: The Rise and Fall of the Woman Air Force Service Pilots (WASPs) of World War II* (New York, 1998). The Madison Square Garden rally was orchestrated by journalist Tex McCrary. See Sherman Adams interview, COHC. On McCrary, see

Charles J. Kelly, *Tex McCrary: Wars, Women, Politics: An Adventurous Life Across the Twentieth Century* (Falls Village, CN, 2009). Some of Eisenhower's own recollections are in Ferrell, ed., *Eisenhower Diaries,* 214.

22. *NYT* (Jan. 17, 1952); Ferrell, ed., *Eisenhower Diaries,* 214. Eisenhower, *Mandate for Change,* 20–21; Picket, *Eisenhower Decides to Run,* 170.

23. Eisenhower Diary, (Feb. 12, 1952), EP, Eisenhower Library. Eisenhower's entry the day before (Feb. 11, 1952) is equally telling: "[T]he performance at the Garden is not only something to make an American fervently proud—it is something that increases his humility, his sense of his own worthiness to fulfill the spoken and unspoken desires and aspirations of so many thousands of [supporters]." Eisenhower Diary (Feb. 11, 1952), *ibid.* See also Eisenhower to Edward Hazlett (Feb. 12, 1952), EP, Pre-presidential Papers, 1916–1952, Principle File, Box 56, Eisenhower Library. And Griffith, *Ike's Letters to a Friend,* 98–99.

24. Eisenhower to Cochran, (Mar. 10, 1952), Jacqueline Cochran Papers, Eisenhower Campaign Series, Box 2, Eisenhower Library.

25. Robinson to Eisenhower (Mar. 14, 1952), Robinson Papers, 1932–1969, Box 2, *ibid.*

26. *Ibid.*

27. Brownell interview, ELOHC.

28. *NYT* (Jan. 8, 1952). See also George Lodge (son of Henry Cabot Lodge), "The Campaign to Win the Presidential Nomination for Dwight D. Eisenhower," (Nov. 16, 1951–July 12, 1952), unpublished manuscript in EP, Papers as President, 1953–1961 (Ann Whitman Files), Admin. Series, Eisenhower Library; and text of Eisenhower's January 7, 1952 statement "regarding his political course" in Robinson Papers, 1932–1969, Box 2, Eisenhower Library. See also *Time* (Jan. 14, 1952).

29. Brownell (probably more than anyone) saw this in Eisenhower's decision to run in this period. See Brownell interview, ELOHC. And Brownell, *Advising Ike,* 100.

30. *NYT* (Feb. 16, 1952).

31. Lodge to Adams (Jan. 4, 1952), EP, Papers as President, 1953–1961 (Ann Whitman Files) Admin. Series, Box 23, Eisenhower Library. See also Adams, *First-Hand Report,* 25. And Adams interview, COHC.

32. *NYT* (Jan. 5, 1952).

33. Ferrell, ed., *Eisenhower Diaries,* 209. Eisenhower made a similar statement to his brother, Milton, in late February. See Dwight to Milton Eisenhower (Feb. 23, 1952), EP, Pre-presidential Papers, 1916–1952, Box 174, Eisenhower Library.

34. Memorandum, Robinson to Lodge, et al. (Jan. 28, 1952), Robinson Papers, 1932–1969, Box 2, Eisenhower Library.

35. *Time* (Feb. 11, 1952).

36. Philip Grant, "The 1952 Minnesota Republican Primary and the Eisenhower Candidacy," *Presidential Studies Quarterly* (summer, 1979), 311. See also Sherman Adams interview, COHC. Edward Stettendahl was on the ballot as a stand-in for MacArthur. He received less than 22,000 votes. On Harold Stassen as a stalking horse for Eisenhower, see Chester Pach and Elmo Richardson, *The Presidency of Dwight D. Eisenhower* (Lawrence, KN, 1991), 18–19.

37. Lodge to Eisenhower (July 16, 1951) in "Personal Interview with General Eisenhower," Lodge Papers, MHS.

38. *Time* (Mar. 24, 1952).

39. Eisenhower Diary (Feb. 25, 1952), EP, Eisenhower Library. For the MacArthur announcement, see *NYT* (Feb. 24, 1952).

40. Eisenhower Diary (Feb. 13, 1953), EP, Eisenhower Library.

41. *NYT* (April 8, 1952); *Time* (April 21, 1952).

42. *NYT* (April 12, 1952). Brownell feared that Taft would win in New Hampshire and take the nomination by default. See also Brownell interview, ELOHC.

43. *NYT* (April 30, 1952). For a reference to Eisenhower's personal letter to Truman, see *ibid.,* (April 30, 1952).

44. *Time* (June 9, 1952).

45. *NYT* (June 16, 1952). Eisenhower references the speech in *Mandate for Change,* 34. A transcript of the speech is in (June 15, 1952), EP, Speeches, Box 1 (Ann Whitman Files), Eisenhower Library. See also New York *Herald-Tribune* (April 13, 1952).

CHAPTER 4

1. Robert L. Dennison to Walt Rostow (Aug. 8, 1972), Robert L. Dennison Papers, Correspondence File, Box 1, Truman Library.

2. The Press Secretary was Eben Ayers. See Eben Ayers Diary (April 2, 1952), Eben Ayers Papers, Box 21, Truman Library. See also Truman interview (Jan. 9, 1952), HSTP, "Mr. President" File, President's Secretary's File, Box 225, Truman Library.

3. Alonzo L. Hamby, *Man of the People: A Life of Harry S. Truman* (New York, 1995), 504–05.

4. The best source on these scandals is, Robert H. Ferrell, *Harry S. Truman: A Life* (Columbia, MO, 1994), 358.

5. Clark Clifford (with Richard Holbrooke), *Counsel to the President: A Memoir* (New York, 1992), 283.

6. Robert H. Ferrell, ed., *Off the Record: The Private Papers of Harry S. Truman* (New York, 1980), 177–78. Truman, *Memoirs,* II, 488–89.

7. *NYT* (Sept. 9, 1953).

8. Clifford, *Counsel,* 281–82. The case was *Youngstown Sheet and Tube Co. vs Sawyer.*

9. Charles Murphy to Robert L. Dennison (Aug. 18, 1972), Dennison Papers, Correspondence File, Box 1, Truman Library; Clifford, *Counsel,* 182.

10. Arthur Krock, *Memoirs: Sixty Years on the Firing Line* (New York, 1968), 267–68. Perhaps the best explanation of this (and whether it occurred or not) is in Ferrell, *Truman,* 448–49, see note 34.

11. Harry S. Truman, "Longhand notes" (July 7, 1952), HSTP, Box 282, Longhand Notes File, Truman Library. See also Ferrell, ed., *Off the Record,* 260–61.

12. *NYT* (Jan. 11, 1952).

13. *NYT* (Feb. 1, 1952); *Public Papers of the Presidents; Containing the Public Messages, Speeches, and Statements of the President* (Washington, DC, 8 vols): *Eisenhower, 1952–1953*, 132. See also *Life* (Feb. 18, 1952). The New Hampshire primary was March 11.

14. A good source on the political differences between Truman and Stevenson is *Life* (Mar. 24, 1952). See page 133.

15. David McCullough, *Truman* (New York, 1992), 891. See also McKeever, *Adlai Stevenson,* 179. Ball, *The Past Has Another Pattern,* 113–16; Robert Dallek, *Harry S. Truman: 33rd President, 1945–1953* (New York, 2008), 140; Martin, *Adlai Stevenson of Illinois,* 521–25; Truman, *Memoirs,* II, 491–92. Ball had set up an "information center" for Stevenson's possible campaign in their law offices in Chicago. He worked to raise several thousand dollars for the cause, and tried to maintain a dialogue between Truman and Stevenson. Martin, *Adlai Stevenson of Illinois,* 533–34.

16. Ferrell, ed., *Off the Record,* 245. For Stevenson's feelings on the response, see Stevenson to Mrs. Edison (Jane) Dick, in Johnson, ed., *Papers of Adlai Stevenson,* 538.

17. Martin, *Adlai Stevenson of Illinois,* 524–25. For more on this meeting, see McKeever, *Adlai Stevenson,* 179.

18. Martin, *Stevenson of Illinois,* 537.

19. Truman, *Memoirs,* II, 555. Ferrell, ed., *Off the Record,* 245.

20. Martin, *Adlai Stevenson of Illinois,* 538.

21. Truman, "Longhand Notes" (July 7, 1952), HSTP, Longhand Notes File, Box 281, Truman Library.

22. Clifford, *Counsel,* 283. For Kefauver in New Hampshire, see *NYT* (Mar.12, and 13, 1952).

23. *Time* (Mar. 31, 1952).

24. Hamby, *Man of the People,* 604.

25. Ball, *The Past Has Another Pattern,* 114–15.

26. Stevenson to Murphy (Mar. 17, 1952) in Johnson, ed., *Papers of Adlai Stevenson,* 532–35.

27. Included were Chief Justice Vinson, speechwriter and advisor Sam Rosenman, Truman's correspondence secretary, Bill Hasset, Truman's Special Counsel Charles Murphy, White House Special Assistant John Steelman, and Clifford.

28. Clifford, *Counsel,* 283.

29. Murphy interview, HSTLOHC. See also Robert J. Donovan, *Tumultuous Years: The Presidency of Harry S. Truman, 1949–1953,* (New York, 1982), 396; Charles Murphy to Robert L. Dennison (Aug. 18, 1972), Dennison Papers, Correspondence File, Box 1, Truman Library. Clark Clifford recounts this meeting in mid-February. But by most other accounts, the meeting occurred in late March. Clifford, *Counsel,* 283.

30. *Life* (Mar. 24, 1952).

31. *NYT* (Mar. 30, 1952).

32. Truman, "Longhand notes," (July 11, 1952), HSTP, Longhand Notes File, Box 282, Truman Library. See also Truman, *Memoirs,* II, 492. For other recollections, see Eben Ayers (Mar. 29, 1952), Ayers Papers, Ayers Diary, Box 21, Truman Library. And *Time* (April 7, 1952).

33. "Meet the Press Transcripts," (May 25, 1952), Lawrence Spivak Papers, Library of Congress.

34. See three letters, Stevenson to Arthur Altschul, Jack Blatt, and Vern Brotherton (all July 11, 1952), Adlai Stevenson Papers, 1952 Presidential Campaign Series, Box 223, Princeton. All three letters include the phrase: "I still pray that I am able to extricate myself and continue on a job which seems to me important . . . to both Illinois and the Democratic Party."

35. See particularly, Speech Files, Stevenson Papers, Box 25, Princeton.

CHAPTER 5

1. *NYT* (Jan. 24, 1952); *Life* (Feb. 4, 1952). Kefauver had allowed his name to be entered in the Illinois primary even before he announced.

2. *NYT* (Dec. 5, 1951).

3. *NYT* (Aug. 8, 1948); *Harper's* (Jan. 1949).

4. Charles L. Fontenay, *Estes Kefauver: A Biography* (Minnetonka, MN, 1980).

5. Perhaps the best source on this is contemporary. See "Mr. Costello's Hands," *St. Louis Post-Dispatch* (Mar. 16, 1957), and New York *Herald-Tribune* (Mar. 27, 1957).

6. Estes Kefauver, "Congressional Reorganization," *The Journal of Politics* (Feb. 1947), 96–107.

7. *Newsweek* (Feb. 4, 1950). A good source on Truman's dislike of Kefauver, is Merle Miller, *Plain Speaking: An Oral Biography of Harry S. Truman* (New York, 1973), 349. Before making use of Miller's *Plain Speaking*, see Robert H. Ferrell and Francis H. Heller, "Plain Faking?" *American Heritage* (May–June, 1995), 14, 16. According to Ferrell and Heller, Miller fabricated some parts of *Plain Speaking*.

8. *Life* (Feb. 4, 1952). Here, *Life* calls Stevenson "the real fair-haired Fair Dealer and the White House choice to cut down Cousin Estes."

9. Joseph and Steward Alsop, "Matter of Fact," *Washington Post* (April 7, 1952). Kefauver did have a big victory in California. He beat state Attorney General Pat Brown and even out polled the Republican favorite son, Earl Warren, and took California's sixty-eight delegates to the Chicago convention.

10. *NYT* (Nov. 9, 1950). Russell received many letters asking him to run for his party's majority leader. He often returned letters explaining that he disagreed with the Truman administration "on many of their policies." See Russell to G.P. Martin (Jan. 3, 1951), Richard Russell Papers, Dictation Files, Box 7, University of Georgia, Athens, GA. Russell to John Sparkman (Nov. 22, 1950), *ibid*. And Russell to Mrs. Mary James Cotterell, *ibid*.

11. Gilbert C. Fite, *Richard B. Russell, Jr.: Senator from Georgia* (Chapel Hill, NC, 1991), see particularly, chapter 13.

12. Russell to W.R. Hughes (Oct. 9, 1951), Russell Papers, Dictation Files, Box 7, University of Georgia. Russell to W.R. Hughes (Oct. 9, 1951), in *ibid*. Russell wrote similar letters to others. See particularly, letters to Henderson Lanham (Sept. 6, 1951); E. McDonald (May 11, 1951); Rollie C. Hudson (May 11, 1951); and Lamar Rutherford Lipscomb (Mar. 10, 1951), all in *ibid*.

13. Donaldson, *Truman Defeats Dewey*, 190; *Pittsburgh Courier* (Dec. 13, 1948); *Chicago Defender* (Nov. 13, 1948). An NAACP postelection survey showed that 69 percent of all African Americans in the nation's major cities voted for Truman. See Henry Lee Moon, "What Chance for Civil Rights," *Crisis* (Feb. 1949), 42–45. See also comprehensive election results in *NYT* (Dec. 11, 1948). Truman, however, denied that the African American vote had been the key to his victory, insisting that it was the votes from organized labor that pushed him over the top in many of the same states where he had won a large majority of black votes.

14. Russell to Governor Johnston Murray (Mar. 31, 1952), Russell Papers, General Correspondence, Box 3, University of Georgia.

15. Fite, *Russell*, 272. By April 1952, however, the ADA had turned against Russell. See "Let's Look at the Record of Senator Richards B. Russell," (April 3, 1952), Stevenson Papers, 1952 Campaign Series, Box 213, Princeton. Here the ADA recounts Russell's votes against foreign aid, organized labor, civil rights, civil liberties, and even against the welfare of the nation's natural resources. By some accounts, Russell had become more conservative in the immediate postwar years.

16. Fite, *Russell*, 289.

17. The Supreme Court case was *U.S. v. California, 332 U.S. 19*. See also Robert Gramling, *Oil on the Edge: Offshore Development, Conflict, and Gridlock* (Albany, NY, 1995), *passim.*

18. "Russell Announcement of Candidacy" (Feb. 28, 1952), Russell Papers, Political Files, Box 193, University of Georgia. More accessible copies can be found in the national press. See particularly, *Washington Post* (Feb. 29, 1952); *NYT* (Feb. 29, 1952).

19. *Time* (Mar. 10, 1952).

20. *Life* (Mar. 24, 1952). Russell constantly insisted that he was not running for Vice President. One good example is *Washington Post* (Mar. 31, 1952).

21. Russell to Jonathan Daniels (Mar. 28, 1952), Russell Papers, General Correspondence, Box 8, University of Georgia. Russell often called the FEPC "socialism." See *New Republic* (May 12, 1952).

22. Russell to Kefauver (April 3, 1952), Russell Papers, Political Files, Box 165, University of Georgia.

23. Russell Campaign Plan for Florida Primary (April 1, 1952), Russell Papers, Political Files, Box 154, University of Georgia.

24. Fontenay, *Estes Kefauver*, 172–74.

25. *Ibid.*, 201–04; Fite, *Russell*, 286–87.

26. Kefauver to Russell (June 19, 1952), Russell Papers, Political Files, Box 185, University of Georgia.

27. Russell to Kefauver (July 20, 1952), *ibid.*

28. Russell to (constituent) Larry Sheats (Oct. 24, 1952), Russell Papers, Political Files, Box 153, University of Georgia. This is an example of several such letters from Russell to various constituents in response to requests that he work for the Stevenson campaign.

29. Despite Russell's desire to portray himself as a national candidate, he often spoke of his racist beliefs. See particularly, interview in *New Republic* (May 12,

1952); and question and answer "Quizzing Russell," *US News and World Report* (June 13, 1952). Stevenson's proposal to end the Senate filibuster is recounted in the candidate's speech before the Democratic and Liberal Party State Convention in New York. *NYT* (Sept. 29, 1952).

30. Russell to H.E. Wolfe (Sept. 3, 1952), Russell Papers, Box 153, University of Georgia; Russell to Ed. R. Russell, *ibid.* And Russell to Otho E. Falls (Sept. 4, 1953), *ibid.*

31. Fite, *Russell*, 333. Gary Donaldson, *First Modern Campaign: Kennedy, Nixon, and the Election of 1960* (Lanham, MD, 2007), 32–33. Kefauver and Albert Gore of Tennessee also did not sign the document. See George Reedy interview, LBJOHC. By some accounts, Strom Thurmond conceived of the Southern Manifesto.

32. See *NYT* for this (Mar. 30, 1952). The Nebraska primary was on April 1.

33. John Robert Greene, *The Crusade: The Presidential Election of 1952* (Lanham, MD, 1985), 123.

34. In his memoirs, Truman wrote that he had told Harriman before the convention that "If it came to a showdown between [Harriman] and Stevenson, I was committed to Stevenson." See, Truman, *Memoirs*, II, 494. On Harriman, see Rudy Abramson, *Spanning the Century: The Life of W. Averell Harriman, 1891–1986* (New York, 1992), 490–500.

CHAPTER 6

1. See Gary A. Donaldson, *The Secret Coalition: Ike, LBJ, and the Search for a Middle Way in the 1950s* (New York, 2014), *passim.*

2. See Gary A. Donaldson, *Liberalism's Last Hurrah: The Presidential Campaign of 1964* (Armonk, NY, 2002) 294–95.

3. Donaldson, *Secret Coalition*, 120–22.

4. Probably the best work on the Dixiecrat movement is Kari Frederickson, *The Dixiecrat Revolt and the End of the Solid South, 1932–1968* (Chapel Hill, NC, 2001). See also William D. Bernard, *Dixiecrats and Democrats: Alabama Politics, 1942–1950* (University, AL, 1974). Donaldson, *Truman Defeats Dewey*, 163. For Humphrey's own analysis of these events, see Hubert Humphrey, *The Education of a Public Man: My Life and Politics* (Minneapolis, MN, 1991); see particularly, chapter 17.

5. A good source on this is Earl Black and Merle Black, *The Rise of the Southern Republicans* (Cambridge, MA, 2002). This is graphed out in a number of places. See particularly pages 271 and 371.

6. Donaldson, *First Modern Campaign*, 156; V. O. Key, *Southern Politics in State and Nation* (New York, 1949), *passim.* See also Earl Black and Merle Black, *Politics and Society in the South* (Cambridge, MA, 1987), 3–72.

7. Theodore C. Sorensen, *Kennedy* (New York, 1965), 216. Sargent Shriver interview "Kennedy's Call to King," John F. Kennedy Library, Boston.

8. Donaldson, *First Modern Campaign*, 156; Theodore White, *The Making of the President, 1960* (New York, 1961), 359; Key, *Southern Politics, passim.* See also Black and Black, *Politics and Society*, 3–72.

9. *NYT* (Nov. 23, 1960). Had African Americans cast their votes in 1960 the same as they had in 1956, Kennedy would most likely have lost Illinois, New Jersey, Michigan, South Carolina, and Delaware. See White, *Making of the President, 1960,* 424.

10. Donaldson, *Truman Defeats Dewey,* 189, 207, 214–15, 220; Steven F. Lawson, *Black Ballots: Voting Rights in the South, 1944–1969* (New York, 1976), 120.

11. See *The Taft Story,* (n.d.), campaign pamphlet; and Bill McAdams to Clarence Brown, "Confidential Memo," titled "Outline of Public Relations and Publicity Program," n.d. (fall1947?), both in Taft Papers, Political Files, Library of Congress. See also James T. Patterson, *Mr. Republican: A Biography of Robert A. Taft* (Boston, MA, 1972), 396–99.

12. Donaldson, *Liberalism's Last Hurrah,* 247–51.

13. David Halberstam, *The Fifties* (New York, 1993), 225–32; Ambrose, *Eisenhower,* II, 347. Donaldson, *First Modern Campaign,* 158.

CHAPTER 7

1. *NYT* (July 3, 1952 and July 7, 1952); Parmet, *Eisenhower,* 80–82.

2. Taft complained of this in his own version of the Fair Play incident. See Robert A. Taft, "Analysis of the Results of the Chicago Convention," (n.d.) Taft Papers, Political Files, Box 431, Library of Congress. He writes here, "The press was completely unfair in their treatment of it." See also Tom Coleman to Clarence Brown (July 14, 1952), *ibid.,* Box 435, Library of Congress. Coleman writes "The greatest handicap that we had was the vicious propaganda conceived by Herb Brownell and supported by the left wing press to make people believe that Senator Taft . . . had no integrity." *NYT* referred to the RNC operating behind an "iron curtain." *NYT* (July 7, 1952).

3. Even if Taft had won all the delegates, he would still have been short of a first ballot victory by nearly 65 votes.

4. Quoted in *Time* (July 14, 1952); and *NYT* (July 7, 1952).

5. *NYT,* (July 5, 1952). See also Parmet, *Eisenhower,* 84–85; Lodge, *Storm Has Many Eyes,* 115–18.

6. Lodge, *Storm Has Many Eyes,* 115–18. See also Hagerty interview, COHC.

7. *NYT* (July 8, 1952). See also William Manchester, *American Caesar: Douglas MacArthur, 1880–1964* (Boston, 1978), 820–21. Manchester called it the "worst speech of MacArthur's career."

8. Brownell, *Advising Ike,* 117, 119; *Time* (July 21, 1952); *NYT* (July 10, 1952); Smith, *Dewey,* 593. Dirksen later apologized for the outburst.

9. Thomas C. Reeves, *The Life and Times of Joe McCarthy: A Biography* (Lanham, MD, 1997), 423.

10. *NYT* (July 10, 1952).

11. Quoted in Reeves, *Life and Times of Joe McCarthy,* 426.

12. *NYT* (July 10, 1952).

13. Quoted in Reeves, *Life and Times of Joe McCarthy,* 427.

14. Brownell, *Advising Ike,* 119; Paul T. David, Malcolm Moos, and Robert Goldman, *Presidential Nominating Politics in 1952* (Baltimore, MD, 1954), 95–97.

15. *Wall Street Journal,* (July 12, 1952); Patterson, *Mr. Republican,* 558.

16. Taft, "Analysis of the Results of the Chicago Convention," *passim.*

17. Hagerty interview, COHC. Eisenhower was quoted in *NYT* as saying that "Taft is a very great American." *NYT* (July 12, 1952); Patterson, *Mr. Republican,* 562–63; and in Brownell, *Advising Ike,* 120.

18. Adams, *First-Hand Report,* 43–44.

19. Herbert S. Parmet, *Richard Nixon and His America* (Boston, MA, 1990), 92; Smith, *Dewey,* 584; Herbert Brownell interview, ELOHC; Richard M. Nixon, *The Memoirs of Richard Nixon* (New York, 1978), 83–84.

20. Hagerty interview, COHC. For another (and probably more complete) list of the players, see Brownell, *Advising Ike,* 121–22. And Adams, *First-Hand Report,* 43.

21. Brownell interview, ELOHC. See also Hagerty interview, COHC.

22. Reeves, *Life and Times of Joe McCarthy,* 371–74. Joseph McCarthy, *America's Retreat from Victory: The Story of George Catlin Marshall* (New York, 1951).

23. Nixon, *The Memoirs of Richard Nixon,* 81–82.

24. See Bert Andrews (journalist, photographer), notes (Sept. 22, 1952), Nixon Papers, Pre-presidential Series, Correspondence files, Box 3, Nixon Library, Loma Linda, CA. Andrews states that Eisenhower referred to Nixon as a "model public servant [whom he] likes very much."

25. See Nixon speeches quoted in *NYT* (Aug. 1, 1952).

26. See Nixon Speeches (Oct. 13, 1952), Stevenson Papers, 1952 Presidential Campaign Series, Box 22, Princeton.

27. From a speech made by Nixon in Pomona, California (Sept. 17, 1952), Nixon Papers, Speech Files, Pre-presidential Series, Box 9, Nixon Library.

28. From a speech by Nixon in Hartford, Connecticut (Sept. 4, 1952), *ibid.*

29. From a speech by Nixon in Boston, Massachusetts (Sept. 7, 1952), *ibid.*

30. Ferrell, ed., *Off the Record,* 260–61.

31. Stevenson, handwritten statement (July 4, 1952), Stevenson Papers, 1952 Campaign Files, Box 26, Princeton.

32. Walter Johnson, *How We Drafted Adlai Stevenson* (New York, 1955), 54.

33. *Chicago Tribune* (July 20, 1952).

34. Johnson, *How We Drafted Stevenson,* 99.

35. *Ibid.,* 100.

36. *NYT* (July 22, 1952).

37. *Ibid.* (Feb. 17, 1952).

38. *Ibid.* (July 20, 1952); Greene, *The Crusade,* 101, 145.

39. *Time* (Aug. 4, 1952).

40. *NYT* (July 7, 1952). Barkley told Truman that if he (Truman) did not run that he (Barkley) would. See Alben Barkley, *That Reminds Me: The Autobiography of the VEEP* (New York, 1954), 224.

41. William Hillman to Truman (July 19, 1952) William Hillman Papers, General File, Box 28, Truman Library. Hillman was a Truman friend, and the editor and writer of several publications attributed to Truman. Hillman told Truman that Barkley was ahead in the pre-vote delegate count, but he could not win the nomination or the election.

42. *Time* (Aug. 4, 1952). For Walter Reuther's look at this, see Reuther to Stevenson (July 29, 1952), Stevenson Papers, Pre-Election Papers, Box 271, Princeton.

43. *NYT* (July 22, 1952). For Barkley's look at this, see Barkley, *That Reminds Me,* 236–37. He refers to this event as the "kiss of death."

44. Perhaps the best accounting of Barkley's speech and the ovation that followed is Eben Ayers Diary (July 23, 1952), Ayers Papers, Box 21, Truman Library. See also Barkley, *That Reminds Me,* 236–37, 241–42; and *Time* (Aug. 4, 1952). The text of Barkley's speech is in *NYT* (July 24, 1952).

45. *NYT* (July 22, 1952). The text of Stevenson's speech is also in this edition. See also Adlai E. Stevenson, *The Major Campaign Speeches of Adlai Stevenson* (New York, 1952), 15–17.

46. The reporter was Anthony Leviero, *NYT* (July 23, 1952).

47. *Ibid.* (July 22, 1952); *Chicago Sun-Times* (July 21, 1952).

48. *NYT* (July 22, 1952). Senator Blair Moody of Michigan placed the loyalty oath before the convention at 12:35 A.M. See Fontenay, *Estes Kefauver,* 216–18.

49. *Ibid.*, 220.

50. Both Arthur Krock articles are in *NYT* (July 25, 1952). See also Joseph B. Gorman, *Kefauver: A Political Biography* (New York, 1971), 151.

51. A text of the platform is in *NYT* (July 24, 1952).

52. *Ibid.* (July 20, 1952).

53. On Truman's health, see "Notes on Meeting with Harry Truman" (July 18, 1952), Hillman Papers, General File, Box 28, Truman Library.

54. Eben Ayers Diary (July 18, 1952) Ayers Papers, Box 21, Truman Library.

55. *Time* (April 7, 1952).

56. Greene, *The Crusade*, 492; Fite, *Russell*, 296; John P Goldsmith, *Colleagues: Russell and Johnson* (Macon, GA, 1998), 29.

57. Truman, *Memoirs* II, 497.

CHAPTER 8

1. *NYT* (Sept. 28, 1952). The Democratic National Committee had negotiated TV time as early as December 1951 (long before Stevenson was nominated) with the theme "Twenty Years of Achievement Under Democratic Administrations." Frank McKinney, "Final Report to the DNC," unpublished manuscript (Aug. 20, 1952), HSTP, Official Files (200–04), Trip File, Truman Library. See also *Time* (Aug. 4, 1952). And, Kathleen Hall Jamieson, *Packaging the Presidency: A History and Criticism of Presidential Campaign Advertising* (New York, 1996), 68.

2. *NYT* (July 30, 1952).

3. *Ibid.*

4. Eisenhower, *Mandate for Change*, 64; Patterson, *Mr. Republican*, 572–73. Ambrose, *Eisenhower*, I, 541–43. Not all observers believe that Eisenhower needed Taft's support. Conservatives, they argue, would have voted for Eisenhower in any case. See particularly, Harris, *Is There A Republican Majority?*, 173. And, Jean Edward Smith, *Eisenhower in War and Peace* (New York, 2012), 530–31.

5. *NYT* (Sept. 9, 1952).

6. Hamilton to Taft (Aug. 27, 1952), Taft Papers, Political Files, Box 452, Library of Congress.

7. Taft to Welker (Aug. 18, 1952), *ibid.*, Subject Files, Correspondence with Senators, 1952, Box 1184, Library of Congress.

8. Taft to Dirksen (Aug. 6, 1952), *ibid.*, Special Files, Box 1286, Library of Congress. See a similar letter from Taft to John D.M. Hamilton (Sept. 4, 1952), *ibid.*, Political Files, Box 452, Library of Congress.

9. Patterson, *Mr. Republican,* 574–75; Parmet, *Eisenhower,* 128–30; Eisenhower, *Mandate for Change,* 64; *Time* (Sept. 22, 1952); *NYT* (Sept. 12, 1952). Taft's press release is in Taft Papers, Special Files, Box 1286, Taft Papers, Library of Congress. The idea that Dewey would not serve in an Eisenhower administration came from Jack Martin. See Martin to Taft (July 25, 1952 and Aug. 14, 1952). Both letters in Taft Papers, Special Files, Box 1286, Library of Congress. Ambrose, *Eisenhower,* I, 553. For a strong narrative account of the meeting, see Smith, *Eisenhower in War and Peace,* 531.

10. Taft to Eisenhower (Oct. 31, 1952), Taft Papers, Subject Files, Box 1106, Library of Congress. Eisenhower, in *Mandate for Change,* writes that Taft gave thirty speeches in nineteen states. See page 64.

11. Taft to Eisenhower (Oct. 31, 1952), Taft Papers, Subject Files, Box 1106, Library of Congress. There were some mistakes in the polling. See Harris, *Is There A Republican Majority?,* xi. This comes from the book's "Forward," written by Paul Lazarfeld and Samuel Stouffer.

12. *Time* (Sept. 15, 1952).

13. See particularly, *NYT* (Oct. 5, 1952 and Nov. 3, 1952). Just before the election, *Newsweek* reported that as many as 13 percent of the electorate was undecided. *Newsweek* (Nov. 3, 1952). A Crossley Poll in *US News and World Report,* gave the undecided vote at just over 11 percent. *US News and World Report* (Oct. 31, 1952).

14. For much of Eisenhower's campaign schedule, see *NYT* (Aug. 31, 1952 and Sept. 15, 1952). James Hagerty has had a great deal to say about Eisenhower's reception in the South. See Hagerty interview, COHC.

15. Henry Cabot Lodge, "Personal Interview with General Eisenhower" (July 16, 1951), Lodge Papers, Lodge-Eisenhower Correspondence, Box 1, MHS.

16. *Time* (Sept. 1, 1952); *Public Papers of the Presidents, Truman, 1952–1953,* 530–31.

17. Ferrell, ed., *Off the Record,* 226–67.

18. Brownell interview, ELOHC.

19. *NYT* (June 16, 1952). One of Eisenhower's most prolific speechwriters, Emmet John Hughes, takes up this topic. See John Emmet Hughes, *The Ordeal of Power* (New York, 1963), 116. Hughes writes: Eisenhower "rebelled against rhetoric. He distrusted abstractions. He shied away from generalizations."

20. Hagerty interview, COHC.

21. *Ibid.*

22. Harris to McBlair (Aug. 8, 1952), Anastos to Schlesinger (Sept. 16, 1952), and Batt to Schlesinger (Oct. 16, 1952), Stevenson Papers, all three letters in Presidential Campaign Series, Box 215, Princeton.

23. Alistair Cooke, *Six Men: Charles Chaplin, H.L. Menkin, Humphrey Bogart, Adlai Stevenson, Bertrand Russell, Edward VIII* (New York, 1977), 136.

24. Even though Eisenhower was himself bald. See Greene, *Crusade*, 173. See also note, page 283.

25. *NYT* (Sept. 16, 1952).

26. *Ibid.*

27. For the *New York Post* story, see (Sept. 18, 1952), and *Time* (Sept. 29, 1952). The story was broken by Leo Katcher, the *Post*'s West Coast correspondent. There is some evidence that a contributor to the fund opposed Nixon for vice president and leaked the story. See Robert Humphreys to Murray Chotiner (Sept. 23, 1952), Nixon Papers, Correspondence Files, Pre-Presidential Series, Box 3, Nixon Library. The *Post* headline read, "Secret Nixon Fund." The next day, the *Post* headline read, "Dick's Own Welfare State." *New York Post* (Sept. 19, 1952). For the Maryville speech, see (Sept. 19,1952), Nixon Papers, Pre-presidential Papers, Speech Files, Box 10, Nixon Library.

28. Nixon often made this point. Stevenson had used the phrase in a letter to the *Portland* (Oregon) *Journal*. But Nixon often added in his speeches that "I will clean it up." See "Pomona Speech" (Sept. 17, 1952), Nixon Papers, Pre-presidential Series, Speech Files, Box 9, Nixon Library. Nixon delivered the Pomona Speech the day before the slush fund article was published in the *New York Post*.

29. *NYT* (Sept. 20, 1952).

30. *New Republic* (Sept. 29, 1952).

31. Brownell interview, ELOHC

32. *NYT* (Sept. 20, 1952).

33. Statement by Nixon (Sept. 21, 1952), Nixon Papers, Pre-presidential Series, Speech Files, Nixon Library. Nixon may well have believed that Eisenhower wanted him to resign. See Nixon, *Memoirs*, 97–98.

34. Memo of Eisenhower-Nixon telephone conversation (Sept. 20, 1952), Nixon Papers, Pre-presidential Series, Correspondence Files, Box 3, Nixon Library. See also Nixon, *Memoirs*, 97–98; Nixon, *Six Crises*, 99–101; Parmet, *Eisenhower*, 136.

35. Dewey to Nixon (Sept. 20, 1952), Nixon Papers, Pre-presidential Papers, Correspondence Files, Box 3, Nixon Library.

36. *NYT* (Sept. 28, 1952). The report came from a Republican furniture manufacturer named Kent Chandler.

37. *NYT* (Sept. 28, 1952). An audit of the Stevenson fund is in *US News and World Report* (Oct. 10, 1952). See also Martin, *Adlai Stevenson of Illinois*, 691–98. And, *NYT* (Sept. 25, 1952). Here, *NYT* writer Arthur Krock calls Stevenson a "hypocrite."

38. *NYT* (Sept. 28, 1952).

39. *Ibid.* (Sept. 19, 1952.

40. *Ibid.* (Sept. 28, 1952).

41. There are a number of sources for the "Checkers" speech. The speech and Nixon's own handwritten notes are in Nixon Papers, Pre-presidential Series, Speech Files, Box 10, Nixon Library. Perhaps the most accessible source for the speech is Richard M. Nixon, *Six Crises* (Garden City, NY, 1962), 113–17. See also *Newsweek*

(Oct. 6, 1952). See *US News and World Report* (Oct. 3, 1952) for an in depth analysis of the Nixon fund, including those who donated to the fund. A copy of the Gibson, Dunn and Crutcher report is in Nixon Papers, Pre-presidential Papers, Speech Files, Box 10, Nixon Library. And in Paul Hoffman Papers, Eminent Personages Files, Box 28, Truman Library. Hoffman headed the Independent Citizens Committee for Eisenhower.

42. See particularly, *NYT* (Sept. 24, 1952).

43. Eisenhower to Nixon (Sept. 23, 1952 10:46 P.M.), Nixon Papers, Pre-presidential Series, Correspondence Files, Box 3, Nixon Library.

44. Parmet, *Eisenhower,* 139.

45. Nixon, *Memoirs,* 106; Nixon, *Six Crises,* 120–21.

46. *NYT* (Sept. 28, 1952).

47. *Ibid.*

48. Nixon campaign press release (Sept. 24, 1952), Nixon Papers, Pre-presidential Series, Correspondence Files, Box 3, Nixon Library. See also Telegram, Dana Smith to Nixon (Sept. 24, 1952) in *ibid.*

49. Field Poll (Oct. 2, 1952), *ibid.,* Box 4, Nixon Library.

50. *NYT* (Sept. 28, 1952).

51. Thomas Amlie to Arthur Schlesinger, Jr., (n.d., 1952), Stevenson Papers, Presidential Campaign Series, Box 215, Princeton Amlie was a Democratic Party insider from North Dakota.

52. *NYT* (Oct. 5, 1952).

53. Parmet, *Eisenhower,* 127. *Time* (Oct. 13, 1952). McCarthy's book was published in 1951 by Devan-Adgin.

54. Hughes, *Ordeal of Power,* 38–41. Parmet, *Eisenhower,* 127–28. See also Eisenhower, *Mandate for Change,* 317–19. Truman called Eisenhower a "coward" for not denouncing McCarthy. See Miller, *Plain Speaking,* 134. Stevenson said that "the pillorying of the innocent has caused the wise to stammer." See Stevenson, (Oct. 8, 1952), Stevenson Papers, Speeches, Box 39, Princeton. Eisenhower's own explanation of all this is in Eisenhower to Harold Stassen (Oct. 5, 1952), EP, Papers as President (Ann Whitman Files) Administration Series, Box 34, Eisenhower Library. And Adams interview, COHC.

55. See particularly, Parmet, *Eisenhower,* 131. Sherman Adams refers to "a brief reference." Adams, *First-Hand Report,* 41.

56. *Ibid.,* 40; Eisenhower, *Mandate for Change,* 318; Reeves, *Life and Times of Joe McCarthy,* 438. Apparently, it was Adams who pushed Eisenhower to drop the criticism of McCarthy. See Adams, *First-Hand Report,* 40.

57. Adams, *First-Hand Report,* 41.

58. *NYT* (Oct. 4, 1952). Reeves, *Life and Times of Joe McCarthy,* 439. Adams, *First-Hand Report,* 40–43; Parmet, *Eisenhower,* 131–32.

59. Adams, *First-Hand Report,* 42.

60. *NYT* (Oct. 4, 1952). See Adams, *First-Hand Report,* 41; Eisenhower, *Mandate for Change,* 318.

61. *NYT* (Oct. 9, 1952); Martin, *Adlai Stevenson of Illinois,* 713; Ambrose, *Eisenhower,* I, 567.

62. Reeves, *Life and Times of Joe McCarthy*, 441–42.

63. *NYT* (Sept. 20, 1952).

64. *Ibid.* (Sept. 23, 1952); Hughes, *Ordeal of Power*, 29–30.

65. *NYT* (Sept. 28, 1952).

66. *Ibid.*

67. *Ibid.*, (Oct. 3, 1952).

68. *Ibid.*, (Oct. 25, 1952). See also *Time* (Nov. 3, 1952).

69. Adams, *First-Hand Report*, 51.

70. A good analysis of the Menard State Prison riot is *Life* (Nov. 10, 1952).

71. Martin, *Adlai Stevenson of Illinois*, 403–404.

72. Fite, *Russell*, 297; Greene, *Crusade*, 214.

73. *Ibid.*, 214.

74. *NYT* (Aug. 5, 1952); Harris, *Is There A Republican Majority?*, 176.

75. *NYT* (Sept. 29, 1952).

76. Martin, *Adlai Stevenson of Illinois*, 650-51; *Time* (Sept. 1, 1952); *NYT* (Sept. 29, 1952).

77. Nixon speech (Aug. 25, 1952), Nixon Papers, Speech Files, Pre-presidential Series, Box 9, Nixon Library.

78. For Eisenhower's personal opinion on the Tidelands issue, see Eisenhower to Lodge (May 20, 1952), Lodge Papers, Lodge-Eisenhower Correspondence, Box 1, MSHS. Here, Eisenhower says he has read the original treaty between Texas and the United States, and notes that "it makes specific mention of tidelands and guarantees their possession to Texas." See also *Washington Post* (June 19, 1952). Eisenhower made a number of speeches in New Orleans on the Tidelands issue. See *New Orleans Times-Picayune* (Oct. 14, 1952); *Time* (Oct. 27, 1952); and Eisenhower, *Mandate for Change*, 206.

79. *NYT* (Aug. 25, 1952). See also O. Douglas Weeks, *Texas Presidential Politics in 1952* (Austin, Texas, 1953), 85. Martin, *Adlai Stevenson of Illinois*, 650–51.

80. Johnson to Stevenson (Sept. 8, 1952), Lyndon B. Johnson Archives, Stevenson Files, Box 9, Johnson Library, Austin, Texas. For more on the situation in Texas, Shivers, and the approaching election see James Lanigan to George Ball (Aug. 20, 1952), Stevenson Papers, 1952 Presidential Campaign Series, Box 213, Princeton. See also *Houston Post* (Aug. 29, 1952). A good analysis of Texas politics in this era is Randall B. Woods, *LBJ: Architect of American Ambition* (Boston, MA, 2007), 248. For LBJ's part in Stevenson's Texas campaign, see George Reedy, JBLOHC, 78. The best source on the Tidelands issue is Gramling, *Oil on the Edge*.

81. Jamieson, *Packaging the Presidency*, 44.

82. Rosser Reeves, "PROGRAM TO GUARANTEE AN EISENHOWER VICTORY, (n.d.), Rosser Reeves Collection, WSHS, Madison.

83. "20-Second TV Announcement," Ted Bates and Company Advertising (Oct. 17, 1952), *ibid.*

84. *NYT* (Sept. 16, 1952)

85. *Ibid.*, (Sept. 16, 1952).

86. Records were not kept on the amounts spent in these years, so there are no records. There are, however, assumptions. See Jamison, *Packaging the Presidency*,

44. Malcolm Moos has determined that $140 million was spent by both parties in 1952. See Moos, *The Republicans* (New York, 1956), 493.

87. *The New York Times* endorsed Eisenhower in late October, 1951. A good source for the battle of the newspapers is Jamison, *Packaging the Presidency*, 57.

88. Harris, *Is There A Republican Majority?*, 125–26, 136; Lubell, *The Future of American Politics*, 245.

89. Angus Campbell, George Gurin, and Warren E Miller, "Television and the Election," *Scientific American* (May, 1953), 47.

90. Harris, *Is There A Republican Majority?*, 60–81.

91. See Robert Divine, *Foreign Policy and US Presidential Elections, 1952–1960* (New York, 1974), 84–85.

92. Louis Harris discusses what he calls the "White-Collar Tide" in his *Is There A Republican Majority?* See pages 125–39.

93. Campbell, *et. al.*, *Voter Decides*, 53–58.

94. Lubell, *The Future of American Politics*, 248.

95. *NYT* (Nov. 8, 1952).

96. Harris, *Is There A Republican Majority?*, 204. Twelve of thirteen "Old Guard Republicans" in the Senate ran behind Eisenhower.

97. Memorandum, (n.d., Nov.–Dec., 1952), Johnson Papers, Senate Files, 1952, Johnson Library.

98. No author, (n.d.), Stevenson Papers, 1952 Presidential Election Files, Box 229, Princeton.

99. Reedy to Johnson (Nov. 6, 1952), Johnson Papers, Senate Office Files, Box 413, Johnson Library.

100. *NYT* (Nov. 6, 1952).

101. Harris, *Is There A Republican Majority?*,173; *NYT* (Nov. 6, 1952). Iowa went for Eisenhower in 1952, but had supported Truman four years earlier.

102. The Arvey quote is in Harris, *Is There A Republican Majority?*, 124. See also Greene, *Crusade*, 225.

103. Alexandra Kendrick, *Prime Time: The Life of Edward R. Morrow* (Boston, MA, 1969), 352.

Bibliography

BOOKS AND ARTICLES

Abramson, Rudy. *Spanning the Century: The Life of W. Averell Harriman. 1891–1986*. New York: William Morrow, 1992.

Adams, Sherman. *First-Hand Report: The Inside Story of the Eisenhower Administration*. London: Hutchenson Publishers, 1962.

Ambrose, Stephen. *Eisenhower*, 2 vols. New York: Simon and Schuster, 1983–1984.

Ball, George W. *The Past Has Another Pattern: Memoirs*. New York: Norton, 1982.

Barkley, Alben. *That Reminds Me: The Autobiography of the VEEP*. New York: Doubleday, 1954.

Bernard, William D. *Dixiecrats and Democrats: Alabama Politics, 1942–1950*. University, Alabama: University of Alabama Press, 1974.

Black, Earl, and Merle Black. *Politics and Society in the South*. Cambridge, Massachusetts: Harvard University Press, 1987.

Black, Earl, and Merle Black. *The Rise of the Southern Republicans*. Cambridge, Massachusetts: Harvard University Press, 2002.

Blum, John Morton, editor. *The Price of Vision: The Diary of Henry A. Wallace, 1942–1946*. New York: Houghton Mifflin, 1973.

Bradley, Omar. *A Soldier's Story*. New York: Henry Holt, 1951.

Broadwater, Jeff. *Adlai Stevenson and American Politics: The Odyssey of a Cold War Liberal*. New York: Twayne, 1994.

Brownell, Herbert (with John P Burke). *Advising Ike: The Memoirs of the Attorney General*. Lawrence, Kansas: University of Kansas Press, 1993.

Burns, James MacGregor. "Is Our Two-Party System in Danger?" *New York Times Magazine* (Sept. 7, 1952), 13, 54, 56.

Butcher Harry C. *My Three Years with Eisenhower: The Personal Diary of Captain Harry C. Blutcher, USNR*. New York: Simon and Schuster, 1942–1949.

Campbell, Angus, et al. "Television and the Election." *Scientific American*. (May, 1953), 46–48.

Campbell, Angus, et al. *The Voter Decides: A Study of the Voter's Perceptions, Attitudes, and Behaviors . . . Based on a Survey of the 1952 Election.* New York: Row, Peterson, 1954.

Clifford, Clark (with Richard Holbrooke). *Counsel to the President: A Memoir.* New York: Random House, 1992.

Cooke, Alistair. *Six Men: Charles Chaplin, H.L. Menkin, Humphry Bogart, Adlai Stevenson, Bertrand Russell, Edward VIII.* New York: Random House, 1977.

Dallek, Robert. *Harry S. Truman: 33rd President, 1945–1953.* New York: Times Books, 2008.

David, Paul T. Malcolm Moos, et al. *Presidential Nominating Politics in 1952.* Baltimore: Johns Hopkins University Press, 1954.

Divine, Robert. *Foreign Policy and US Presidential Elections, 1952–1960.* New York: New Viewpoints, 1974.

Donaldson, Gary A. *First Modern Campaign: Kennedy, Nixon, and the Election of 1960.* Lanham, Maryland: Roman and Littlefield Press, 2007.

Donaldson, Gary A. *Liberalism's Last Hurrah: The Presidential Campaign of 1964.* Armonk, New York: M.E. Sharpe Press, 2003.

Donaldson, Gary A. *The Secret Coalition: Ike, LBJ, and the Search for a Middle Way in the 1950s.* New York: Carrell, 2014.

Donaldson, Gary A. *Truman Defeats Dewey.* Lexington, Kentucky: University of Kentucky Press, 1999.

Donovan, Robert J. *Tumultuous Years: The Presidency of Harry S. Truman, 1949–1953.* New York: Norton, 1982.

Dubovsky, Melvyn and Warren Van Tyne, *John L. Lewis: A Biography.* Urbana, Illinois: University of Illinois Press, 1986.

Eisenhower, Dwight D. *Crusade in Europe.* Garden City, New York: Doubleday, 1948.

Eisenhower, Dwight D. *Mandate for Change: 1953–1956.* Garden City, New York: Doubleday, 1963.

Ferrell, Robert H. *Harry S. Truman: A Life.* Columbia, Missouri: University of Missouri Press, 1994.

Ferrell, Robert H. editor. *Off the Record: The Private Papers of Harry S. Truman.* New York: Penguin, 1980.

Ferrell, Robert H. editor. *The Eisenhower Diaries.* New York: Norton, 1981.

Ferrell, Robert H. and Francis H. Heller. "Plain Faking?" *American Heritage* (May–June, 1995), 14, 16.

Fite, Gilbert C. *Richard B. Russell, Jr.: Senator from Georgia.* Chapel Hill, North Carolina: University of North Carolina Press, 1991.

Fontenay, Charles L. *Estes Kefauver: A Biography.* Minnetonka, Minnesota: Olympic Marketing Corporation, 1980.

Forrestal, James. *Forrestal Diaries.* New York: Viking, 1951.

Frederickson, Kari. *The Dixiecrat Revolt and the End of the Solid South, 1932–1968.* Chapel Hill, North Carolina: University of North Carolina Press, 2001

Galambos, Louis, Alfred D. Chandler, Jr. et al., editors. *The Papers of Dwight D. Eisenhower.* 21 vols. Baltimore: Johns Hopkins University Press, 1970–2001.

Galbraith, John Kenneth. *A Life in Our Times.* New York: Houghton Mifflin, 1982.

Gillon, Steven M. *Politics and Vision: The ADA and American Liberalism, 1947–1985.* New York: Oxford University Press, 1987.

Goldsmith, John P. *Colleagues: Russell and Johnson.* Macon, Georgia: Mercer University Press, 1998.

Gorman, Joseph B. *Kefauver: A Political Biography.* New York: Oxford University Press, 1971.

Gramling, Robert. *Oil on the Edge: Offshore Development, Conflict, and Gridlock.* Albany, New York: State University of New York Press, 1995.

Grant, Phillip. "The 1952 Minnesota Republican Primary and the Eisenhower Candidacy," *Presidential Studies Quarterly.* (Summer, 1979), 311–15.

Greene, John Robert. *The Crusade: The Presidential Election of 1952.* Lanham, Maryland: University Press of America, 1985.

Griffith, Robert. "Dwight D. Eisenhower and the Corporate Commonwealth," *American Historical Review.* (Feb. 1982), 87–122.

Griffith, Robert. *Ike's Letters to a Friend.* Lawrence, Kansas: University of Kansas Press, 1984.

Gunther, John. *Eisenhower: The Man and the Symbol.* New York: Harper and Row, 1952.

Halberstam, David. *The Fifties.* New York: Villard, 1993.

Hamby, Alonzo L. *Man of the People: A Life of Harry S. Truman.* New York: Oxford University Press, 1995.

Harold F., Alonzo. *Beyond the New Deal: Harry S. Truman and American Liberalism.* New York: Columbia University Press, 1973.

Harris, Louis. *Is There A Republican Majority? Political Trends, 1952–1956.* New York: Harper and Brothers, 1954.

Hughes, John Emmet. *The Ordeal of Power.* New York: Dell, 1962.

Humphrey, Hubert. *The Education of a Public Man: My Life and Politics.* Minneapolis, Minnesota: University of Minnesota Press, 1991.

Jamieson, Kathleen Hall. *Packaging the Presidency: A History and Criticism of Presidential Advertising.* New York: Oxford University Press, 1996.

Johnson, Walter. *How We Drafted Adlai Stevenson.* New York: Knopf, 1955.

Johnson, Walter, editor. *The Papers of Adlai Stevenson, Governor of Illinois, 1949–1953.* Boston: Little, Brown, 1973.

Johnson, Walter, editor. *The Papers of Adlai Stevenson, Washington to Springfield, 1941–1948.* Boston: Little, Brown, 1973.

Jordan, David M. *FDR, Dewey, and the Election of 1944.* Bloomington, Indiana: Indiana University Press, 2011.

Kefauver, Estes. "Congressional Reorganization." *The Journal of Politics.* (Feb. 1947), 96–107.

Kelly, Charles J. *Tex McCrary: Wars, Women, Politics: An Adventurous Life Across the Twentieth Century.* Falls Village Connecticut: Hamilton Books, 2009.

Kendrick, Alexandra. *Prime Time: The Life of Edward R. Morrow,* Boston: Little, Brown, 1969.

Key, V.O. *Southern Politics in State and Nation.* New York: Vintage, 1949.

Krock, Arthur. *Memoirs: Sixty Years on the Firing Line.* New York: Funk and Wagnall's, 1968.

Lawson, Steven F. *Black Ballots: Voting Rights in the South, 1944–1969.* New York: Columbia University Press, 1976.

Lee, R. Alton. *Truman and Taft-Hartley: A Question of Mandate.* Lexington, Kentucky: University of Kentucky Press, 1966.

Leuctenburg, William E. *In the Shadow of FDR: From Harry Truman to Ronald Reagan.* Ithaca, New York: Cornell University Press, 1989.

Lodge, Henry Cabot. *The Storm Has Many Eyes: A Personal Narrative.* New York: Norton, 1973.

Lubell, Samuel. *Revolt of the Moderates.* New York: Harper and Brothers, 1956.

Lubell, Samuel. *The Future of American Politics.* New York: Greenwood, 1964.

Lyon, Peter. *Eisenhower: Portrait of a Hero.* Boston: Little, Brown, 1974.

Manchester, William. *American Caesar: Douglas MacArthur, 1880–1964.* Boston: Little, Brown, 1978.

Martin, John Bartlow. *Adlai Stevenson of Illinois.* Garden City, New York: Doubleday, 1976.

McCann, Kevin. *Man From Abilene: Dwight Eisenhower, A Story of Leadership.* Garden City, New York: Doubleday, 1952.

McCarthy, Joseph. *America's Retreat from Victory: The Story of George Catlin Marshall.* New York: Devin-Adair, 1951.

McCullough, David. *Truman.* New York: Simon and Schuster, 1992.

McKeever, Porter. *Adlai Stevenson: His Life and Legacy.* New York: William Morrow, 1989.

Merryman, Molly. *Clipped Wings: The Rise and Fall of the Woman Air Force Service Pilots (WASPs) of World War II* New York: New York University Press, 1998.

Miller, Merle. *Plain Speaking: An Oral Biography of Harry S. Truman.* New York: Berkley, 1973.

Miller, William J. *Henry Cabot Lodge: A Biography by William Miller.* New York: Heineman, 1967.

Neal, Steve. *Harry and Ike: The Partnership that Remade the Postwar World.* New York: Scribner, 2001.

Nixon, Richard M. *Six Crises.* Garden City, New York: Doubleday, 1962.

Nixon, Richard M. *The Memoirs of Richard Nixon.* New York: Grosset and Dunlap, 1978.

Parmet, Herbert S. *Eisenhower and the American Crusade.* New York: Macmillan, 1972.

Parmet, Herbert S. *Richard Nixon and His America.* Boston: Little, Brown, 1990.

Patch, Chester and Elmo Richardson. *The Presidency of Dwight D. Eisenhower.* Lawrence Kansas: University of Kansas Press, 1991.

Patterson, James T. *Mr. Republican: A Biography of Robert A. Taft.* Boston: Little, Brown, 1972.

Pickett, William. *Eisenhower Decides to Run: Presidential Politics and Cold War Strategy.* Chicago: Ivan R. Dee, 2000.

Public Papers of the Presidents; Containing the Public Messages, Speeches, and Statements of the President. Washington, DC: National Archives and Records Service.

Reeves, Thomas C. *The Life and Times of Joe McCarthy: A Biography.* Lanham, Maryland: Madison Books, 1997.

Seidman, Joel. *American Labor from Defense to Reconversion.* Chicago: University of Chicago Press, 1953.

Smith, Jean Edward. *Eisenhower in War and Peace.* New York; Random House, 2012.

Smith, Richard Norton. *Thomas E. Dewey and His Times.* New York: publisher, 1982.

Sorensen, Theodore C. *Kennedy.* New York: Harper and Row, 1965.

Steel, Ronald. *Walter Lippmann and the American Century.* Boston: Little, Brown, 1980.

Stevenson, Adlai E. *The Major Campaign Speeches of Adlai Stevenson.* New York: Random House, 1952.

Truman, Harry S. *Memoirs,* 2 vols, Garden City, New York: Doubleday, 1955–1956.

Weinstein, Allen. *Perjury: The Hiss-Chambers Case.* New York: Alfred Knopf, 1978.

White, Theodore. *The Making of the President, 1960.* New York: Antheneum, 1961.

White, William S. *The Taft Story.* New York: Harper, 1954.

Woods, Randall B. *LBJ: Architect of American Ambition.* Boston: Harvard University Press, 2007.

ARCHIVAL COLLECTIONS

Americans for Democratic Action Papers, Wisconsin State Historical Society, Madison, Wisconsin

Eben Ayers Diary, Harry S. Truman Papers, Harry S. Truman Library, Independence, Missouri

Edwin N. Clark Papers, Eisenhower Library, Abilene, Kansas

Jacqueline Cochran Papers, Eisenhower Library

Robert L. Dennison Papers, Truman Library

Dwight D. Eisenhower Papers, Eisenhower Library, Abilene, Kansas

Dwight D. Eisenhower Diary, Eisenhower Papers, Eisenhower Library, Abilene, Kansas

William Hillman Papers, Harry S. Truman Library, Independence, Missouri

Lyndon B. Johnson Papers, Lyndon B. Johnson Library, Austin, Texas

Lyndon B. Johnson Archives, Lyndon B. Johnson Library, Austin, Texas

Henry Cabot Lodge, Jr. Papers, Massachusetts Historical Society, Boston, Massachusetts

Richard M. Nixon Papers, Richard M. Nixon Library, Loma Linda, California

William Robinson, Jr. Papers, Dwight D. Eisenhower Library, Abilene, Kansas

Richard Russell Collection, Russell Library, University of Georgia

Lawrence Spivak Papers, Library of Congress, Washington, DC

Adlai E. Stevenson Papers, Mudd Library, Princeton University, Princeton, New Jersey

Robert A. Taft Papers, Library of Congress, Washington, DC

Harry S. Truman Papers, Harry S. Truman Library, Independence, Missouri

Index

About the Author

Gary A. Donaldson is the Keller Foundation Chair in American History at Xavier University in New Orleans. His other books include *The First Modern Campaign: Kennedy, Nixon, and the Election of 1960; Liberalism's Last Hurrah: The Presidential Campaign of 1964; Dewey Defeats Truman*; and *America At War Since 1945*, among others. He lives in Mandeville, Louisiana.